SPRINT THE CRAWL

Harry Gallagher

SPRINT THE CRAWL

Harry Gallagher

with a special chapter on
U.S. sprint performances
by Buck Dawson

Pelham Books

First published in Great Britain by
PELHAM BOOKS LTD
52 Bedford Square,
London WC1B 3EF
1976

ISBN 0 7207 0905 9
Filmset and printed in Great Britain by
BAS Printers Limited, Wallop, Hampshire

Contents

Illustrations

Foreword

by *Dr. Paul P. Hauch, Honorary Secretary, Fédération Internationale de Natation Amateur*

Harry Gallagher ranks high among the benefactors of amateur swimming throughout the world. Through previous publications, and now in this volume, he shares with readers the pearls of wisdom which overflow from a limitless reservoir of research and experience.

Gallagher's insatiable quest for knowledge, his dedication to the coaching profession and his successes in the development of competitors of world prominence, have equipped him well with knowledge and expertise which he willingly offers to swim-conscious people. Many of his former protégés have reached the highest levels as Olympic, world and national champions, Jon Henricks, Dawn Fraser, Brad Cooper, Lyn McClements, Graham White and Steve Holland among them.

Truly an international coach, as his 24 Olympians attest, perhaps his most remarkable feat has been the tutoring of the winners of six Olympic sprint titles, making him the obvious choice to write *Sprint the Crawl.*

A lifetime of teaching and training swimmers and conducting courses for competitors and coaches throughout the world has instilled in him the concept of "Teach them before you train them", and his book is replete with the application of this admirable philosophy.

P.P.H.

Introduction

To a few there is something beautiful about a dedicated swim team, or for that matter any other hard working sporting group. It is not a delicate beauty, it is physical. Across the pool see the lines of graded sprinters race between the multi-coloured lane markers. Young bodies strive, speed and tumble in unison. Forty, fifty or more pounding hearts with hopes rising. All are in the pursuit of excellence, all integrated, and all in friendship.

The more apparent beauties—a slither of light across flashing arms, the muted silence of the breaststroke team moving through a pool of blue, the boys' cheeky faces, the sweetness of the girls—are far outweighed by the beauty of human movement and power which emanate from the well-disciplined squad. Coaching and training have so many frustrating areas that those closely involved are apt to lose sight of the wholesomeness of it all. To the coach dulled by the familiarity of the practices there are many hours when beauty seems far away. To the student things will often appear harsh, but to the uninitiated walking into the stadium and seeing the obvious order of things there is an exciting feeling.

In terms of success or prestige the greatest teams today are tutored by coaches who hold a firm rein. All-time great sprinters from Fraser to Spitz, or even back as far as Weissmuller, have emerged from swim schools where training intelligence has had priority over merciless mileage.

There are often, as in all things competitive, a few fanatics whose desire for unreasonable physical output defies the logic of physiology. Some coaches will exhaust the bulk of the team in order to produce one champion, the one who survives. These coaches seek to immortalise themselves. They rarely, if ever, develop swimmers of note beyond the age of sixteen years, for this is the age when intelligent pupils refuse to accept the dogmatic policies or illogical theories of the unbendable coach.

We are moving into a world of re-cyclables, but worn-out spirits and torn-out muscles rarely come back. They are the disposables. Superior athletes respond best to situations which are favourable to the exposure of their highest quality—not the coach's. This will always be the theme. The in-focus trainer has flexibility. He may be likened to his nylon lane markers—pliable but unbreakable.

The future intrigues us. It is the limitation of our reasoning which restricts our mental projection into the future. In this book I seek only to assess the possibility of man's speed through water, but the future holds levels of achievement beyond our reasoning in all fields. Do not be limited in your thinking. Being limited makes you predictable. If you are predictable you are vulnerable and being vulnerable makes you expendable.

A giant of a mind, Leonardo da Vinci, could visualise extended flight—but to the planets? The athletic nabobs of the 19th century could never have expanded their minds to accept the idea that teenage girls of the 20th century would be able to concede to Captain Webb eight or nine hours start in a race across the English Channel and win. So let us not limit our vision for the impossible is only a matter of time. If a thing appears to be possible then the chances are it will be. Coaches of the future will feed these philosophies into the super sprinters of the 21st century.

The next breakthrough for the main part, will be mental. Not only for the forty-four seconds of the 100 metres super sprint but in the prior years of training and believing. To lift to higher plateaus unshackle the mind and free it from tradition, prejudice. Possess a clear mind upon which your first marks will be targets that no previous coach has had the intellect or courage for which to aim.

The super coaches—yet to emerge—will create but a handful of super-sprinters for as the times tumble the material to work upon will become scarce. Teams will be small. Coach-pupil relationships will be intense and have a singleminded purpose. All will be free from external worries. The super-coaches will work together as a team, but each will be a specialist.

The super sprinters—yet to emerge—will be super Enders, long in stroke, long in stature. Their incentives will be strong and materialistic.

Presentation will have to become professional. We can no longer assemble the finest athletes in the world and display them in a Punch and Judy setting. Meets should be spectaculars.

The confusion of priorities, the acceptance of the artificial, the ever distending softness of the western world all point to the end of an era—an era rooted in the better principles of courage and pioneering. So, trainers and trainees take pride in your contribution to youth. You may be manning one of the last outposts of the Greek Ideal.

To coach is to create and a thing of which to be proud. I know that I feel ten feet tall when I enter the stadium with Wendy Lee. Walk into the swim arena surrounded by your "A" relay team ready to do battle: it is the closest you will ever come to feeling like James Bond.

1. The race

He who wins, of a sudden, some noble prize in the rich years of youth
Is raised high with hope; his manhood takes wings;
He has in his heart what is better than wealth.

PINDAR

The comical hooter despatched the eight superb athletes. It also condoned a cacophony of the multitudinous bells, clappers, whistles and screams from around the giant stadium. The final of the men's one hundred metres freestyle had started. I stood, huddled inconspicuously against a pillar, at the far end of the pool, intermingled with minor Mexican officials and workers. I had it so planned that if my swimmer was beaten I could slip out of the side door unnoticed, tail between my legs so-to-speak, for it's common knowledge that it's the coach who must bear the blame for failures, irrespective of the myriad of uncontrollable circumstances. If you doubt me, ask any Age Group mother.

As you may have gathered I was not exactly full of confidence, but I hoped it did not show through to the members of the Australian Swim Team that I was coaching. A little aside I could see "Doc" Counsilman, the battle-scarred veteran coach of a thousand meets, looking slightly paler than usual. The unflappable Peter Daland appeared jittery, and Sherman Chavoor's complexion was starting to match his hair. To me, under the circumstances, these were comforting observations. For coaches and competitors there is very little pleasure in international competition, especially the Olympics. Being through it before does not make it any easier either, it is always a fresh trauma. I tried to comfort myself by saying "after all it's only a sport, an amateur sport, and who will really care of the outcome a year or even a month from now, except perhaps the competitors and their coaches?". These meets do take a heavy toll on the coaches. Show me a coach who has not had one or more stomach, kidney, lung, leg, back, skin, sleep, weight, alcohol, personality, financial or marital problem during his career and you are presenting me with one who has not coached Olympics.

Australia's Michael Wenden was not the favourite. In fact he was not even listed in the top five or six sprinters in the world, but Mike had lacked top competition, a common ailment in Australia, and above all he was a competitor, one who could lift himself to unpredictable heights under pressure. He was unlike any swimmer I had handled before: stoic, taciturn and so very adult for his seventeen years. Listed in his qualities were great natural strength, complete lack of competitive fear and two of the assets I seek most in champions—commonsense and watersense. My pupils had collected Olympic medals before on previous lucky occasions but they had always been favourites. The odds had always been my way. This final was for me, so different. We had to overcome Mark Spitz, being hailed as the greatest sprinter in the history of the sport; Ken Walsh, the world record holder; and the cream of the European sprinters, all listed ahead of Mike.

Mike had done his "homework" well. He had rarely missed a training session, he had taken pains to keep his body weight steady, executed his swim sprints at almost full speed. He had never neglected his land exercise programme, never sidestepped the kick sprints that he hated, and made sure that he was never beaten in the workouts. The sum of all these benefits gave hope that we could succeed even if Mike was not the fastest man in the race, for often it is the fittest man that wins the medal, and the fastest man may not necessarily be the fittest.

I have spent many hours in the stand watching Mike's rivals in their training workouts. My stopwatches clicked overtime. I looked for strong points, sought weaknesses, considered possibilities. In training, Zachary Zorn was undoubtedly the fastest man on earth over a short distance, the Andy Coan of the '68s, but his finish was suspect. It was also rumoured that he had been weakened by the gastro-intestinal illness, "Montezumas curse". Mark Spitz appeared to have a "dead spot" just after the turns and we were sure that he had a respiratory infection aggravated by the altitude. Ken Walsh impressed me as a very clever rival. I cannot assess the worth of these spying sessions but they were invaluable in cementing coach-pupil relationships at the highest level, and at the most opportune moment. Of course most coaches worth their salt keep a tab on the opposition and some go to extreme measures, but I have never been able to verify if, as is rumoured, the Russians employ observers who lip read, through binoculars, the conversations between rival coaches and their pupils.

Our racing plan was simple enough. Instructions in a sprint should never be complicated, there is not enough time for detail, should be no room for dilemma. The scheme was based in part on one of Johnny Weissmuller's proven principles. I never look at my competitors during a race—if I do I lose concentration on what I'm supposed to be doing. The only time I did digress from this golden rule, I was almost beaten, quipped "Tarzan", back in 1927. Mike was not to be influenced by others; he had to swim his own race one hundred per cent. We had conjectured that the three Americans, old rivals, would watch each other closely and that they and the Russians would make moves and appropriate counter moves through the fifty-two second scramble.

Mike had to sprint hard down the first twenty-five metres in order to nullify the mediocrity of his start, to make sure that the leaders did not create an unassailable "break". The effectiveness of Mike's turn was also doubtful so we planned that some distance out from the wall he would increase to maximum speed. We hoped that the others might be easing back a fraction in order to negotiate the turn with a minimum of risk, for no one can chance a muffed turn in the final of an Olympic sprint. Off the turn we were going to hold maximum pressure. We assumed that the very fast beginners would now be starting to feel the pinch, and that the eight thousand feet altitude would not be helping them much either. The fifty-metre mark was also Mike's danger zone—technically. He had the habit of shortening his stroke, over revving and losing his grip on the water. He had to concentrate on holding form, stretching out further in front, thrusting back just a little more and thinking of the power pull-push at all costs. On the home run he had to maintain this stroke and give it his all, never looking left or right, just a superhuman explosion of power in which he was to completely drain himself. It was to be a gamble—pitting strength against the finer techniques of his rivals. The foregoing probably appears complex but in essence Mike's racing plan boiled down to "Go out fast—hit that turn hard—get your stroke 'right' after the push off, then when you feel set, give it all you have all the way home."

The sports medicine staff had indicated that there was little likelihood of any world records at that altitude—eight thousand feet—especially after heats and semi-finals, so we had planned a solo swim to win, and not for time. Mike approached the final with the utmost confidence.

We had used the usual gimmickry during the preliminaries: a fairly heavy workout just before the heats, just enough to take a little of the edge from Mike's sparkle. A heavy swim suit for the heats and semi-finals, no body or leg shaving till after the "semis"! Above all there was to be no unnecessary mental sweat before the finals, only one psychological peak. Mike was to swim marginally just inside times that would guarantee his reaching the final.

For a micro-second the world's fastest swimmers were suspended in perfect flight above the pool, then with a convulsive thump they landed. Zorn, like a man possessed, immediately broke away from the others. I have never seen such acceleration. With incredible ease he outstripped the cream of the world's sprinters. Spitz looked like a novice. Walsh and Wenden were last as Zorn zipped past the twenty-five metre mark in eleven short seconds. If I had been squeamish before the event I was now positively ill. I had sadly miscalculated Zorn's opening gambit for he was now three metres ahead of Mike, and that's a long way in twenty-five. Spitz shot a hurried glance at Zorn but he must have known that Zac was not the man to beat, for he seemed quite unruffled by the early break.

At the forty-metre mark things started to happen. The overmuscled Russians, Illichev and Kulikov, increased their rating simultaneously. Bobby McGregor and Mark Spitz held their fire as Wenden and Walsh tried to close the gap. Zorn hit the fifty-metre end first, then there was a flurry of feet and foaming bodies as the rest of the swimmers gyrated. Spitz managed a terrific tumble, as did Walsh. Mike fumbled around with his unorthodox way of changing direction and as he surfaced I knew he had a chance—a place medal at least, for although he came out of the turn last, his first few strokes were fresh and fast. Near the seventy-metre mark Zorn's earlier indiscretions took their toll and he stopped as if caught in a vortex. His 24·4 sec. for that first fifty metres had been his undoing. He had gambled everything on tear-away tactics to upset his rivals and he had lost. The Russians were now starting to struggle, Nicolao could not find a finish and Wenden, McGregor and Walsh went past them in a straight line. But Spitz had outfoxed them all for he had started his final run a fraction earlier and now he took the lead.

Mike started his shot for home. Inch by inch Spitz started to lose his sting. I do not know what inner strengths accumulate and release in a superman's mind and body at such moments; it's beyond my ken to understand how such powers can be released upon command, when the human frame is apparently exhausted, but whatever the ingredients Mike Wenden had them in abundance that night. His rugged stroke changed gears. His rating increased to an even higher pitch and he started to lift over the water. Never have I seen a swimmer ride higher in a race. He virtually ripped across the surface. His kick was thrashing but it was suspect; his arms and shoulders were all powerful. Fifteen metres from the end his devastating finish inched him into the lead and like a true champion he never yielded. He crashed into the finish pad a fraction of time ahead of the fast-finishing Walsh. Spitz was third. I hurried to the locker room and was violently ill, unaware that the Aussie had set a new world and Olympic record of 52·2 sec.

Sometime after the presentation I managed to push my way through to the bemedalled Mike.

"Well how was it, boy?" I quizzed.

"Great," answered Mike, blessing me with one of his rare grins.

"What did you think of the race plan?" I said, puffing out my ego a little and waiting for the compliment. Mike looked a trifle sheepish.

"To be quite truthful I just couldn't follow it when I got my sights on the leaders in the last lap I made a real old fashioned race out of it. I chased them all the way."

What could I say? I said nothing. I was bedazzled by that large gold medal around Mike's neck.

Sometime later, before the final of the medley teams relay, Mike mumbled something about "I might try it your way this time." He did. I think. I was never quite confident enough to ask him. Nevertheless his "split" of 51·4 sec. was phenomenal whichever way he did it. To me, at the time of writing it is still equal to the present world record of 49·99 sec. created at sea level.

Why describe this race, even though it was an exciting Olympic final? It has been duplicated many times before. Because I was involved and because we succeeded it must be one of my favourite events. But more than this. In retrospect I now realise that I learnt and relearnt a lot in those fifty-two seconds. I learnt that 26 sec. plus 26 sec. makes a better total than 24 sec. plus 29 sec. I learnt that if illness strikes at Olympic level your chances are practically nil.

I learnt that dedication to training plus strength can overcome minor shortcomings in technique. I learnt that with intelligent pupils, there must be a "cancel" button that wipes out race instructions when unique circumstances occur.

Let us consider for a moment the following. Eight international finalists with totally different backgrounds, eight varied reasons for seeking success, and over the years eight dissimilar methods of training. The complexity of the combination of factors that influenced these young men to all reach, through diverse routes, the starting blocks of an Olympic final, would be indeed a fascinating study. There are many secrets hidden in such a study, perhaps we will be able to unravel a few of them in the following pages.

As for success one can only guess why the Russians sought it. Watch them at poolside or in the water, they are so very serious; I don't think that they do it for fun. Perhaps a gold medal would have meant minor economic advancement, was it the love of the sport, chauvinism, personal satisfaction, or the way to an easier life? The Americans, why did they seek the laurel wreath? Perhaps in Mark Spitz's case, he had to succeed to save face, not his own so much but that of the United States, for hadn't he been billed as a five gold medal certainty by the American press? When illness struck him his loss of form was inversely proportional to the public pressure upon him. I imagine that in Ken Walsh's case it was the "expected" thing to win, after all he was the world record holder for this distance, and this placed tremendous pressure on his ego. As for Bobby McGregor, the manly Scot, this race was do or die, possibly his last competitive swim. He had narrowly missed the gold medal at Tokyo in 1964 now only the first place would compensate for those four hard years of working and waiting. I know Mike Wenden's main motivator was simply to beat the challenge, purely personal satisfaction, to become non-pariel. This he achieved.

Towards the end of the swimming road the reasons for wishing to succeed are very different from those at the beginning of the swim career. In the early years it is the fun, even just going to the pool, the friendships, the possible side trips, the love of hard work, the poolside chatter, or speaking to the coach, that enslaves the pupil. Once the serious stage has been reached, when a few fairly important races have been won and the point of no return has been reached, then the reasons for succeeding become much more adult. There awakens in the student a greater motivating force than he has ever known before, and possibly greater than anything he will know in his post-competitive life. Most dream of world records or the Olympics and these are the prime movers, but very few will ever admit to it. And what great ideals they are to have. World records and world titles are paragraphs in the book of swimming but Olympic titles are whole chapters. To win that "gold" at the Olympics is a small claim to immortality in sport. Dust may gather on your name but it will never be erased and of course you are in the very elite of company from Epialtes of Rhodes, Diomedes of Athens in 448 B.C. to Spitz of California in A.D. 1972.

2. Sprinters: their qualities, needs, rewards

Perhaps the reward for the spirit who tries
Is not the goal but the exercise.

EDMUND VANCE COOKE

Perhaps all swimmers who gain selection into Olympic teams are men and women of above average sporting ability in the first instance. They are the acme of youth, the arch types, but they are the chosen few. They are outnumbered thousands to one by swimmers who are in training and trying in various degrees of seriousness, but who never make the international swimming circuit. In Australia there are nearly 100,000 people connected with swimming, most of them in some sort of training and all in swim clubs. Australia's Olympic team seldom exceeds 24 swimmers so the odds of winning that green blazer are about one in four thousand; in the United States the odds are even greater. Sprinters of the U.S.A. have one big advantage over their Australian contemporaries however and it is the fact they live in the centre of the swimming world. Australia is isolated from the action.

For those who do not reach world class swimming there can be many fringe benefits, some not always apparent, that will make all the hard work and the time spent worth the effort. The youth who participates in prolonged exercising stints is, by improving the efficiency and quality of his organs and tissues, laying claim to a longer and healthier life. It is a fact that long term trainees can expect a bonus in healthy longevity, accidents excluded. Oarsmen, long distance runners and walkers, skiers, bicycle riders and swimmers are the main beneficiaries in this scheme of nature, the train now–gain later concept. Researchers suggest that the breakdown in condition approximately equals the build-up period, so if you train hard for ten years you can expect up to ten years of better than average condition after training ceases. Since the probability of those twenty years being disease-free is very high, the athlete has set down a very good foundation for later life.

There is strong evidence that the long term swimmer improves his ability to absorb knowledge and to increase his concentration. It could be true that initially "above average" students are attracted to this non-injurious, individual sport, for the school "drop out" is almost unknown on the swim team. In two decades of coaching I have only encountered two swimmers who were world champions and school failures. Invariably once continuous training commences the school grades improve. An overwhelming number of American male Olympic swim finalists are University students. This situation is not repeated in Australia because in the "system" the swimmer has to be a champion before he reaches

University level for there are no coaches and facilities are poor at the Universities. A percentage of the best swimmers eventually find themselves in the pipeline to the U.S. Universities as a consequence.

Parents often remark on their child's improved position in class and especially how much better "organised" they are at home, since majoring in swimming. It appears that the pupil can transfer his bank of concentration and determination acquired from training, to his studies. Physiologists will expound theories that the brain's chemistry is enhanced by a fitter body. Not that the squad resembles a tertulia of savants, they don't, but swimmers are smart and sprinters are smarter.

Commercial, industrial and professional opportunities are "fair game" for retiring swimmers. Perhaps it is because sprinters in the main are extroverts, vigorous in their approach to problems and situations, quick to grasp an opportunity, to "give it a go". Success in business may be their fortune because of the high level of acceptance that the sportsmen have in the commercial world. This table of Australian freestyle sprint champions during the last fifteen years will help to illustrate my statement.

*	1950–1952	Frank O'Neill	Australia's largest swim pool supplier
*	1953–1956	Jon Henricks	Director, American Machinery Company
*	1957–1960	John Devitt	Executive Editor, Speedo International
*	1961–1966	David Dickson	Journalist
*	1967	Greg Rogers	Director, Machine Supply Company
*	1968–1974	Michael Wenden M.B.E.	Economist and University graduate
*	1975	Graham Windeatt	Junior Executive

Overseas travel is one of the more immediate rewards for the top sprinter, and it is fact that more sprinters make more trips than do any other style of swimmer, the ratio being three or four to one, for the sprinters are usually required to make up the relays as well as swim in their individual events. Each season the teams become larger and the trips more frequent. These tours can be a tremendous bonus to the sprinters' education and development (one coach insists that his touring team take in all the art galleries, historical places and geographical features whenever possible). It has been noted that swimmers who have made trips usually move up to a more adult or sophisticated level when choosing friends. Their untravelled contemporaries possibly appear dull.

A side benefit of great importance, although not fully appreciated, is that hard training through the character-forming years of eight to eighteen tends to turn the swimmer away from the present day pitfalls of unacceptable social behaviour, drug taking, smoking. Not that many coaches lecture often or directly against such maladies, it is just that the principles applying in developing a champion sprinter—a fit body and an enquiring mind, correct diet, things in moderation, abstinence from alcohol, adequate rest—suffuses into the pupil's behavioural patterns. This overspread is permanent in some cases, semi-permanent in others. An increasing number of youngsters are being directed into swim teams, track teams, basketball teams, because their parents realise the benefits of team training in character building.

The coach's own life style comes under close scrutiny from very perceptive pupils and it is a strong influencing medium. It is known that a dedicated coach and a happy team can often do more to mould the character of a swim student than the parental or school environment. In cases where the home life is deficient in the presentation of life's priorities many a youth has been put on, or held on the right course by the sobering influence of the coach and the squad. Most coaches of age group swimmers and above, see and communicate with their pupils much more than their parents often do, especially the fathers. It has been estimated in one study, that the coach sees his pupil on the average of 24 hours per week, whereas the executive-type father with weekend sporting interests, has contact with his son or daughter on the average of twelve hours weekly.

For the most part, according to a survey recently carried out by American sociologist, John Kelly, the benefits far outweigh any problems associated with full time swimming training. One fourth of all the mothers interviewed and one third of the fathers did not list any negative aspects at all. Benefits of physical development, learning how to set goals and disciplining one's self to achieve them, and friendships are seen as significant and positive elements in the training team. The tables on page 19 present parental thinking according to the survey.

From the tables it appears that the physical and character-forming bonuses from regular training far outstrip the irksome problems of wasting time and travel.

High school and university scholarships can be a reward to many, for it is a fact that the world's greatest sprinters are bedded down in the universities of the United States, and a fair percentage of these are scholarship students from home and abroad. Sprinters are encouraged by "livewire" university coaches to "sign up" because of their ability to excel over the 100 or even 50 metres freestyle. In the high schools the short sprint is prestigious. Unfortunately no such aura surrounds the Aussie speed man and this is hindering the national sprinting development. I have even heard the super 50-metre men degradingly and erroneously referred to as "speedy squibs" or "gutless wonders".

I have a penchant for sprinters but this is not the general trend. The majority of coaches prefer to train their swimmers on a middle or long distance programme, it is certainly easier. Sprinters require and demand attention but the training of distance swimmers is not so intense. Sprinters are important because they can earn more points in any meet. They are the fun personalities of the team, they keep the coach jumping, the work-

Benefits of swimming	Mother	Father
Physical	71%	60%
Discipline, setting goals	57%	46%
Associations, friends	58%	41%
Self confidence, satisfaction	29%	26%
Competition	24%	22%
Responsibility, maturing	24%	13%
Sportsmanship	23%	16%
Other	16%	19%

Negative side of swimming	Mother	Father
Time consuming, tiring	45%	42%
Team or coach over-competitive	18%	10%
Parents over-competitive	10%	2%
Family schedule problems	10%	7%
Financial cost	4%	1%
Cliques on the team	10%	1%
Other	14%	7%
No negative aspects listed	24%	36%

outs exciting and unpredictable. They banter and barter, they grizzle, groan and grunt. They are super-sensitive, supercilious and superbiate, nevertheless the group is not a team without the sprinters. Perhaps because of the apparent lack of care for sprinters in Australia, the sprint records are starting to mark time, and there is strong evidence that this may be so in the United Kingdom and in Canada as well. The regrettable move by the Olympic Federation of deleting two men's sprint events from future Olympics can only be labelled as pedantic. The 4 × 100 metres men's freestyle relay and the 200 metres individual medley are two spine-tingling events for sprinters and spectators. They are exciting events to train for and their loss from the Olympic calendar could portend the loss of sprinting as a major force in future Games. All nations have these events at their top meets.

The rate of improvement in the world's freestyle sprint records is slowing down. This is to be expected as we approach the "ultimates", but in the men's freestyle the deterioration is alarming. The men's 100 metres has improved 4·78 seconds in the last twenty years but the girls have bettered their 1955 mark by 7·64 seconds. If one is to make modest allowances for technical advances such as no hand touch turns, grab starts, sloping starting blocks, non-turbulent lane markers, adjustable pool water, skin-tight bathers and the larger physique of the present-day champions, *it would appear that a large percentage of the time improvement has come from "refinements" and not from the skill of the stroke per se.*

An overhaul of the stroke mechanics of the sprint, or the setting up of a whole new way of training sprinters, is long overdue. This table shows the slow down in improvement over the last few years. We can expect a spurt forward in Olympic year but there is no possibility of the men's freestyle improving three seconds to line up with the women's gain over the past twenty years.

Men's world records	**100 m. freestyle**	**100 m. butterfly**	**100 m. back stroke**	**100 m. breast-stroke**	**1500 m. freestyle**
1955	55·80	1:01·50	1:02·10	1:08·20	18:19·00
1975	51·12	54·27	56·30	1:03.88	15:20·91
Improvement (seconds)	4·68	7·23	5·80	4·32	2:58.09
Improvement since 1973	0·10	0·0	0·0	0·14	10·94
Women's World Records					**800 m. freestyle**
1955	1:04·60	1:13·10	1:10·90	1:18·10	10:42·40
1975	56·96	1:01·88	1:02·98	1:12·28	8:47·50
Improvement (seconds)	7·64	11·22	7·92	5·82	1:54·90
Improvement since 1973	1·16	·43	2·01	1·30	5·47

It takes a long time, many years of concentrated effort, to reach a peak. There are no exceptions to this rule. Years ago when records were in their infancy, a half dedicated athlete could swim a few miles weekly and with a little luck he might break a record. Training usually extended for three or four months of the year. Not so nowadays. Each succeeding generation has relentlessly pushed the records lower and lower so that it now requires a full time effort by sprinter and coach to create a new, temporary mark.

When one considers that it may take up to 15 per cent of a lifetime to reach that final, competitive swim (not taking into consideration the Masters' competitions) it is obvious that a lot of intelligent applications should be made in the early years of training to see if you have a chance of success. Dr. James Counsilman points out that success comes equally to those who have had early victories and to those who have been denied pre-teenage distinction. This is true but it needs commonsense truthfully to calculate your chances of becoming a champion. It is not logical to train diligently and with single-mindedness of purpose for the sprint for three or four years if, after this time, you are not starting to achieve a modicum of success. There must be some reward. It is no use dreaming of a national title if you cannot make the finals in the local school events. One must be realistic, perhaps you are not a sprinter after all, try the distances, try the other strokes, try water polo, try surf swimming, try synchronised swimming, you may have a niche there somewhere where you will shine. After a prolonged period of concentrated training, if you do not even make a mini mark then turn your energies into something more rewarding. You can still remain with the team if you like the companionship, the sport is very short of beginner coaches and officials and you do not have to be a great swimmer to be a good coach.

There is no chance of reaching the Gold standard unless you have trained longer than seven years. Johnnie-come-lately does not win Olympic medals or open national titles. The average time lies between eight and twelve years of continual training and racing, for the ultimate success, or the top of your personal spire. These years will be thwarted with many reverses, defeats, illnesses, thoughts of quitting. The world's greatest sprinter since Weissmuller, Mark Spitz, has had a lengthy career of such hardships. This should be an inspiration to many. All superior sprinters whom I have coached have had careers dogged with illnesses or just plain "bad luck". The world's finest female sprinter, Dawn Fraser, endured a decade of asthma, hepatitis, muscle injuries, automobile accidents and a three-year disqualification term. These all necessitated long breaks from the training pool. The years of concentrated training to reach their ultimate victory are recorded here with the names of some all-time great sprinters: Jon Henricks (5), John Devitt (10), Don Schollander (11), Michael Wenden (8), Mark Spitz (13).

The two most successful Age Group swimmers in the United States have been Sue Pederson and Gary Hall. Both had long, chequered swim careers based on success, failure, thoughts of giving it all away. They persevered. Hall, an Olympian at Munich, set 10 world records towards the end of his long career. He is now married and recently swam his fastest-ever time for 100 yards butterfly at the age of 23 years. As a 10-year-old he ranked first in a phenomenal 14 events in the Age Group competitions but only ranked first place twice as an 11 and 12-year-old. He then quit swimming but returned to the ranks of the 15 to 17 Age Groups with an outstanding nine first placings. Sue Pederson was ranked first in an unbelievable nineteen events as a 10-year-old and under, taking seventeen firsts in one year. She gained six firsts as an 11 and 12-year-old swimmer but then jumped up to eight firsts in the 13 and 14 year grouping. Finally, in the 15 to 17 age range she managed only two firsts but finished her career with a world record and a trip to the Mexico Olympics.

From this evidence it is apparent that if you have decided to make swimming your number one sport, then it is advisable to stay with it until you have reached your best personal target, and your physiological peak. Therefore, if you are having success take the long term when calculating your prospects. The "consistency" medal must go to the late Sir Frank Beaurepaire of Melbourne, who "placed" at Olympics from 1908 to 1924, after overcoming many hardships. An intelligent appraisal is needed to see if you have reached the top of your swim career. Under normal circumstances, if you have trained hard for a full season and enjoyed good health, if your times have not moved or if they have it is only fractionally, then you must evaluate the worth of putting in another full year. You alone will be able to answer this question honestly.

The structure of the Australian training plan follows these lines:

1. Ages 4 to 7 years, learn to swim at special schools for safety reasons. (90% of the Australian population live on the coastal fringes). Two strokes are taught, freestyle and backstroke. Lessons are one or two per week in small classes.
2. Ages 7 to 10 years, join a mini squad. These squads usually train three to four times per week. Sessions are of one hour. All strokes are taught. Training rarely exceeds 3,000 metres per session with the average closer to 2,000 metres. Advanced pupils in this age group train as much as ten times per week. Join the local swim club. There is still fun in the training.
3. Ages 10 to 13 years, enrol in a full squad under a professional coach. Train 10 to 13 times per week with an average of 4,000 metres per session and up to 40,000 metres per week. Pupils aim to make the national qualifying times. Serious trainees are usually well groomed in all aspects of speed swimming in all the strokes during these years. Coaches set down the long-range targets for the outstanding pupils. Gymnasium or home exercises are introduced. Some pupils commence vitamin supplementation, start recording regularly in their log books. Usually make their first swim trips.
4. Ages 14 to 15 years, the critical years in Australia. Swimmers not showing promise usually move to other interests or sports. This particularly applies to country swimmers. Training is between 10 and 12 times per week with the average workout covering up to 6,000 metres and often totalling 80,000 metres per week. Regular supplementary exercises are carried out. Sprinters should aim to swim within 10 seconds of the world record. School demands are heaviest during these years.
5. Ages 16 years and over, only the champions and near champions are still seriously training after their sixteenth birthday. They are well enough organised by now to cope with the higher schooling demands and the training, but all other sporting activities and some social life is cancelled. A percentage of the boys join surf clubs. This is the stage when improvement must be on the log sheet each season. The average age of swimmers representing Australia internationally is boys 17½ years, girls 15 years. Masters' swimming competition in Australia

is in its infancy.

Bob Mattson, Head Coach, Wilmington Aquatic Club, U.S.A., is a fine organiser. Here is his system to cater for all groups:

1. Sea Serpents, from 3 to 6 years. These groups (10–15 in numbers) work on relaxation, stroke correction, stamina and fun. They meet twice a week for 45 minutes sessions. They swim from 400 to 1200 yards each session. They compete in mini meets at the club.
2. Pre-team, from 6 to 8 years. There are three groups of ascending levels; Sea Tigers, Super Sea Tigers and Golden Sea Tigers. The groups are made up of twenty swimmers. This group undergoes slightly advanced stroking, swim training, stamina and fun. The group meets twice weekly for 60-minute sessions with the assistant coach, Ned Haubein. The competitive scene is stepped up considerably in this group, but basically it is still a swim lesson workout.
3. General Team, from 8 to 13 years. This more serious group practises 7 times per week, with a compulsory attendance of at least three sessions. 120 swimmers are listed on this team but the average attendance is 65 due to the car pool scheduling. Yardage is from 2,500 to 5,000 on weekdays and up to 6,000 on weekends. Head Coach Bob Mattson takes control over the 8 lanes.
4. Senior Squad, from 11 to 20 years. Practice is available seven days a week. Most swimmers attend at least five days with the Super Seniors seven days per week. Bob Mattson takes the 65 swimmers in this group but on the average only 45 attend each workout. Yardage ranges from 4,000 to 10,000.
5. Masters Programme. Special mechanics classes for the parents and other interested adults are held, but most of the veterans work out on their own schedules.

Sprinters need strength. Strength may be defined as the ability to work against resistance. The efficiency of strength depends essentially on the contractile power of the muscular tissue. I have never seen a physically weak swimmer who could perform a really fast 100 metres. Beginner swimmers with a weak musculature may improve rapidly when training commences because gains in strength exceed 50 per cent within the first four weeks when regular exercise is undertaken.

The external musculature of most sprinters seems to point to natural strength. The groups of muscles used for propulsion (and the allied secondary muscles) are easily discernible, even when at rest. Others have to work hard to develop their swimming muscle strength to the required standard. To be able to take a young athlete, and over the years watch him form into a pleasing symmetry of shape and fitness, is one of the more rewarding aspects of sprint coaching. The total action of swimming moulds the youthful torso ideally. The sprint movements are forceful, rapid and have a short rest relaxation period. This causes the musculature to develop rapidly. Shapewise the ideal figure may emerge from doing pool work solely, but the strength needed to be the top man on the team has to be acquired from exercises out of the water. Dawn Fraser was skinny and wiry when she first started training at the age of 13. A well-balanced gymnasium programme gave her shape and strength. Mark Spitz's fine physique is well known to all. Long term exercises out of the water are the reason for this.

Specific strength is needed for sprinting. The muscles that are needed most should be strengthened most. Since the major portion of power for swimming emanates from above the hips, modern strengthening exercise programmes concentrate on this area. Flexibility and streamlining are two requirements for the lower limbs. Cross education (a phenomenon where unexercised muscles are improved a little in strength when muscles near by, or on the other side of the body, are strengthened), plays a role in conditioning minor muscles which are not specifically worked in the gymnasium. The exercise of swimming tones up all voluntary muscles.

In formulating a strength programme care must be taken not to spend time on developing muscles not particularly useful in sprinting. Do not overdo the squat movement unless the thighs and calves are under-developed, avoid exercises that will restrict the range of flexibility in the shoulder or ankle joints. Strength with full-range flexibility and the absence of bulk is the ingredient of a good land schedule. Bulk should be avoided, it restricts flexibility, it uses up a portion of the available blood flow that could be otherwise directed into more valuable employment. Muscle bulk lowers the body's position in the water and creates added resistance. Some over-bulked swimmers have an amazing turn of speed for a very short distance but very quickly the advantages of super strength turn into disadvantages, the bulky muscles puffing up to such dimensions that it is actually painful for the sprinter to continue. Over-bulked sprinters cannot go past the first 50 metres turn, with speed. Once the bulk has been built up by excessive weight training or forced feeding it cannot be reduced in the swimming life-time of the sprinter. Over-bulked sprinters "go to fat" very easily when training is curtailed. Multiple world record holder, Jon Konrads, had the ideal swimming physique when young but had difficulty in maintaining his speed towards the end of his career when his musculature over-bulked. He was a big eater.

The amount of time available usually decrees the composition of the strength programme in the gymnasium. Some successful power schedules have been based on 10 or less specific exercises, especially for the older sprinter, who is usually hard-pressed for extra time in the swim gym. For the sprinter's exercise plan I use flexi-strength (flexibility and firmness). Since sprinters need superior strength, some time must be spent in working with heavy weights or very hard resistances, not a lot, but some. The advantage of using maximal or near maximal weights in strength training is to activate some of the high threshhold neurons that normally would be dormant. Some coaches state that the days of the bar-bell are over and if we use them we are stagnating. This is not so. The fads of today are out of fashion tomorrow only to return once again in due course. Special equipment has its place in the modern swim gym and since most of the machines do a specific job we should use them, if and when we need them, and not as a panacea for all physical requirements. The sound exercise programme will be constructed upon general movements of all-round development for the younger sprinter with a more specialised set of exercises as he matures. Since swimmers fall in categories of crawl, 'flier, dorsal or breaststroke, sprint and distance, individual exercises should be tailored to suit the stroke.

Sprinters need size, or perhaps I should say height is an advantage. Only two sprinters in modern times have been under 5 ft. 11 in. (180 cm.) in winning an Olympic Sprint title. They were Spitz and Schollander.

Of importance is the weight for height ratio. Over 5 per cent overweight or underweight, when using the national standards, places the sprinter in the danger zone of poor performance. To be a top sprinter one must have the physique conforming within narrow limits of weight to height for optimum results. The three main categories of body types who have been successful at sprinting recently are:

* Tall and strong
  Jim Montgomery 6 ft. 5 in. (196 cm.) and 190 lb. (86 kg.)
* Medium and muscular
  Michael Wenden 6 ft. 1 in. (185 cm.) and 168 lb. (76 kg).
* Medium and lithe
  Mark Spitz 5 ft. 10 in. (178 cm.) and 158 lb. (72 kg.)

In women's sprints the tall and medium group clearly has the highest success rate. Shirley Babashoff, Kornelia Ender, Dawn Fraser ranging between 126 and 140 pounds (57 to 64 kg.) when at their peak. Five feet eight inches (173 cm.) seems to approach the ideal height, four of the last five world record holders for the 100 metres freestyle have been within one inch (2·54 cm.) of this mark. Two of the shortest world class sprinters today are Sonya Gray at 5 ft. 4 in. (163 cm.) and 120 lb. (54 kg.) and Kathy Heddy 5 ft. 2 in. (158 cm.) and 130 lb. (59 kg.). Height, weight and strength increase rapidly in females from 9 years to 19 years of age, the growth spurt in males being slightly later at between 12 years and 19 years. Whereas the height growth will slow down from 19 or 20 years, strength and weight will increase. Strength will slowly increase until 30 years of age and then start to decrease. This is why great sprinters have to wait until their strength catches up to their earlier growth spurt before they can produce their fastest times. Weight increase will persist after the age of thirty.

There is a mystique that the alert coach seeks in every new prospective champion. It is speed—naturally; it is to a large extent, unexplainable. Some pupils, but not too many, are able to move through the water fluently and fluidly. They seem to slither, stretch and slide without much apparent effort and yet they speed, not that they appear to have good styles either, in these early stages. The Spanish have a word—*duende*—the word itself is difficult to explain. It's more of a feeling than a word. It means to many Spaniards many things, all good. One thing it does mean is unmistakable class and may be said of a novice matador, who although awkward and unsure, has the mark of greatness upon him. Mattes had it, unexplainable class, a class of unbelievable ease; Fraser had it, ease and grace and speed. Spitz had it in his butterfly. This quality of class makes the task of the sprinter much easier, in training and in competition, if he's fortunate enough to possess it. The records have now reached that point where not only strength, lots of quality mileage and adequate technique are the ingredients for success: tomorrow's champions must have class and *duende*.

If one tends to have slow land movements naturally, it is extremely unlikely that sprinting will be your forte, for once a skill is mastered speed of movement can only be improved minimally by training. It is not so much that great speed of movement is necessary to work the arms and legs in sprinting—after all he only does a few more revolutions of each arm, each pool length, than the distance man. As an example, Shane Gould, who held the world record for the 100 metres and the 1500 metres at the same time, executed 60 strokes in 30 seconds in the second 50 metres of the 100 metres event compared with 55 strokes in 34 seconds for the 50 metres lengths in the 1500 metres race. There is a definable difference however. "Natural" speed is the essential norm in the sprinters complete make-up. He must be sharp. It is the sum total of all his physiological responses and reactions that separates him from the swimmer who is just that fraction slower. It is his higher metabolism, his speedier reflexes, his higher heart rate potential that gives him the slight speed edge that designates him as a sprinter.

The structure of the muscle has important implications on speed. In many muscles of the body there are two kinds of fibres, particularly in the extensors. Call them red fibres and white fibres. Red fibres have colour because they contain muscle haemoglobin, a rich energy source and also a large amount of fat granules. These characteristics are linked with the ability for long or sustained activity. On the other hand, white fibres lack these supplies of energy rich material and consequently can only function for a brief period of time. Inter-related to this difference is the difference in the properties of red and white muscles. White fibres contract much quicker, reach their maximum tension in contraction more rapidly and relax to normal resting state faster than do the red fibres. Because they differ in what they can do they are involved in different kinds of behaviour. In general, flexor muscle fibres are white, extensors red. So the sprinter has white twitch muscle fibres and the endurance swimmer, red. There is nothing we can do about the physiological make-up of our swimmers in this respect but nevertheless we strive for more endurance in our sprinters and more speed in our distance men.

Many times I have seen distance men try to come back down to the 100 metres, trying for extra team points or to fill a relay. The result is invariably mediocre. Catastrophic is the sprinter trying to reach out over the distances. A former pupil, 1500 metres world record holder, Stephen Holland, is incapable of producing speed. Many a beating he has taken from school mates over the shorter distances. Parents and coaches should realise it is becoming increasingly difficult to excel over the complete swimming spectrum. The days will soon be gone forever when swimmers like Gould can hold every world freestyle record concomitantly. At the Mexico Olympics I tried to topple the U.S.A. relay team in the 4 × 200 metres event. The Australian team was composed of two 1500 metres men, a butterfly swimmer and a sprinter. Nevertheless, every swimmer did his best time; I have never seen distance boys so transformed, they were motivated and confident but try as they may they just did not look like speed men. Schollander dived into the last "leg" metres ahead of Wenden and that was the way the teams finished, the sprinters (U.S.A.) first and the non-sprinter team (Australia) second. Sprinters need inherent speed, if you have not go it, there is little you can do about it.

Jack Nelson, Head Coach of the U.S.A. women's team for the 1976 Montreal Olympics, has a fine record as a sprint coach. Recently he was interviewed by *The Journal Herald* and his comments are pertinent to this chapter. Here is a partial list of some of his speedsters.

	100 yards		**100 metres**	
David Edgar	44·5	1971		
Ken Knox	45·1	1973;	51·7	1973
Andy Coan	43·99	1975;	51·23	1974
Ann Marshall	52·13	1974;	59·11	1975
Bonnie Brown	51·13	1975;	59·7	1975

Q—What different approaches are taken to coaching men and women swimmers? How do the motivations differ?

A—Generally, challenge the men and love the women. It's an emotional sport. A woman is made to enjoy being treated nice by a man. It's their nature to work harder, I think, when treated nice. I'm also nice to the guys, but in a different way. I remind them that they have a responsibility to themselves to stand up, fight and be the best in the world. But you can't really generalise. Every woman is different, as is each man. There are many different approaches. They don't all work. The more successful coaches are the ones who guess right more often. All coaches are totally dependent upon the ability of those with whom they work.

Q—How does a swim coach deal with the parents of his competitors?

A—Without the parents to support the swimmer, the coach doesn't have a swimmer. It's a three-way street. Many of us, when we're young, feel we have to fight the parents. Quite the contrary, you've got to work with the parents. You try to convince the parents they shouldn't coach the child, but for goodness sake, there's another 20 hours in the day when the child has to be groomed, trained and raised properly. If you have parents who are intelligent and hungry, it carries over into the mental hungriness of the swimmer. This sport is too tough not to be mentally hungry.

Q—Why are the record times in swimming dropping so dramatically?

A—I don't feel that present day or past day swimmers have gone as fast as they can. A statement generally accepted is that we're getting more athletes into swimming now. We're not just getting the poor little kid on the block who gets sand kicked in his face. We've got some real horses coming into our sport. With the great ability of the athletes, we have to get better times. The coaches' training methods are better, too. The mental acceptance of going faster is better among our young people. But for that matter, what's young? Is 13 (years old) young, or is 23 young? Personally, I think both are young. But if the 23-year-old doesn't think he or she is young, then he or she is not young. Physiological maturity is not always ours prior to chronological maturity, but in a lot of cases it is. When you have a 13-year-old woman doing the same job a 23-year-old is doing, you have the physiological maturity to match the mental maturity.

Q—Was there any turning point for getting the better athletes involved in swimming?

A—It's been a gradual thing. I don't think we can attribute it to any major break-through. There haven't been any female Tarzans or anything like that. If the media would glamorise swimming more, then we would get even faster. The high school football team gets more coverage than the national or Olympic (swimming) team. Every four years, the media finds us, right before we bring home more gold medals than any other athletic team in the Olympics. The word "Olympics" is the magic word. A swimmer can be the best in the world for three straight years, but if he or she fails to make the Olympic team, nobody but other swimmers know about him or her.

Q—Have any new training methods developed in recent years contributed to the lower times?

A—Practically everything "new" is 10 to 40 years old, if not 80. I'd say 99 per cent of those articles we read about new training methods are about something that's been used for years. They give it a name and they write about it.

Q—Is there any forseeable limit to what the records can be lowered to?

A—I don't think so in our lifetime. I don't anticipate any limit right now. For instance, when a man can go 20 seconds in the 50-yard freestyle and only two men are going 43 seconds in the 100, that doesn't make a lot of sense. People were shocked, excited and thrilled when Andy Coan went 43·99—the first human to break 44 seconds in the 100. The American record of 44·5 had been sitting there since 1971. Nobody had gone near it. So bingo, up pops a 16-year-old who goes 43·99. That woke up the college boys so now 44s are abundant. And we had a 21-year-old college man (Alabama's Jonty Skinner) go 43·92, which was even faster. So now it's no big deal to go 44 anymore. But for three years it was the epitome.

Q—Is it conceivable that sometime in the future a top woman swimmer could compete equally on a top men's team?

A—On an equal basis, physiologically, no. Unless there would be some type of physiological phenomenon where men would be born with feminine-type characteristics and women start taking on male characteristics. Our top female athletes can destroy the common man on the street. But top female against top male—running, jumping, swimming, fighting—there's no contest.

Q—What are the differences between the limits of the men and women swimmers?

A—The girls swim quite rapidly, but because of lack of physiological strength on the starts and turns are way behind the boys. But I shouldn't even call them boys and girls. They're men and women. You've got to be a man or woman to get to these nationals . . . you can't do it if you're a boy or a girl. Humans have a knack of catching the carrot that's held out to them. A perfect example is our time standards. Each year, our time standards are dropped and, each year, the swimmers go as fast as they have to. Then they come to the nationals and swim as fast as they have to to get into the finals of the race.

Shirley Babashoff is a great example, I think. She appeared to float through 400 yards of the 500-yard freestyle last night and then took off with a 56 (in the final 100 yards). Shirley Babashoff is so much better than what she had to be last night. If there had been another great swimmer in that race, she might have been pushed to break her own American record. I really feel that some great drops are yet to be made. You will see world records galore in the Olympic Trials in '76. There will be world records in each race, and some of the people breaking the records will not make the Olympic team. We can take only three swimmers in each event, and as a consequence we have some swimmers who could be finalists in the Olympics who will have to sit home and watch it on TV.

Q—Has the growth of women's sports had any noticeable effect on swimming?

A—One thing is absolute: college swimming for women. We've been swimming for years with girls and a few women. Now with college scholarships, we have a chance at more women. We saw a 13-year-old break an American record last night. Now, when they are older, provided they have the same mental attitude, they can be greater. It's kind of normal to get stronger, smarter, more experience. That's why I'm excited about college athletic scholarships for women. Women now have an incentive.

Q—Why do so many swimmers quit competing at a young age?

A—The United States is built around money. It's sad. A sports page should not call itself a sports page. The sports page should put a big dollar sign before P-O-R-T-S and call itself the money page. The more money an athlete gets, the bigger his headline. It doesn't matter if Catfish Hunter hasn't won a game. What matters is that he got $3 million. I'm not criticising him . . . I'd like to see more rich athletes. But I would like to see some of it directed toward swimmers. It costs swimmers money to be great. It costs their parents a bundle. If there was more incentive than just personal satisfaction, I believe you would see more swimmers staying in the sport longer. Even the men retire long before they reach their potential. Swimming is so demanding. You take four hours out of your day (for training) plus the time going to and from practice, and you have five or six hours shot already.

Q—If swimmers haven't reached their psychological limits, why not and what is the limit?

A—If our educators tell us we're only using 5 per cent of our brain, there's 95 per cent left, right? It's unfortunate that the human is a lazy being. The great ones come along every once in a while and absolutely refuse to accept the norm. They go beyond. And then, interestingly enough, those who have been satisfied with the norm look out there and see the great one and start following the shooting star. The time standard required just to qualify for the nationals now would have won the nationals maybe 10 years ago. Like Shirley Babashoff, who went 4·15 in the 400 metres free-style last summer . . . that would have been second or third place in the '60 Olympics in the men's division. (Actually it would have won the event.) The mind is our greatest weapon. It decides our whole existence, our success or lack of success.

Q—What's your forecast for the '76 Olympics?

A—I feel the United States will have a great team. I feel no one can dare predict at this time who that team will consist of. We're going to come out of our Olympic Trials with some super results and go into Montreal to be met by some great swimmers—I'm talking about women now—from Canada, East Germany, Australia, Japan, Hungary and any one of a number of other countries.

3. Some refinements

Endure and persist, this pain will turn to your good in the end.

Ovid

The ingredients for sprinting successes are many and varied. Scores of swimmers with obvious potential have never made the "top ten" or even the "top fifty" lists because of a multiplicity of reasons, some not immediately associated with swimming. In Australia, without a doubt, the major reason is the lack of a coach with experience or enthusiasm within the geographical region of the aspiring champion. Australia is so short of coaches that dozens of swim wizards in the outer suburbs of the great cities are never "discovered" and many hundreds more in the vast country areas never get to first base. It is not uncommon for a pupil to travel upwards of 100 miles a day, in two round trips, to get to a coach or facilities. Lack of finance (and it is becoming an important item), the shortage of available transport, the absence of parental assistance and encouragement, the necessity to forsake serious training for school studies, no all year round training facilities, are just some of the reasons why would-be champions often do not emerge. There is a check list at the end of this chapter that may assist you to assess your chances of success. These pointers are taken from observations, discussions, readings and practice by myself and other coaches, over many years.

Sprinters need endurance and you as a sprint star of the future, should remember this salient point above all others. When the going gets tough, and the endurance is starting to form, you must keep the pressure up, not slide back into a zone of comfort. Most sprinters evolve out of a general squad of youngsters who are, in their earlier years at least, subjected to long sessions of basic work and stroke corrective programming. Because of this, future sprint stars often achieve some success as middle distance performers, or it may be more correct to say that they do not "sparkle" as sprinters in these early years. It was common belief for many years that the best sprinters emerged from the camps where coaches insisted on long distance workouts when the pupils were young. We now know that there are two types of sprinters, the super sprinter and the one hundred metre man. The super sprinter is the one who can thrash the whole team over 25 or 50 metres, he is often great up to 100 yards short course. He never takes the world record for the 100 metres, he never wins the Olympic sprint title—the true 100 metre man does. The super sprinter relies on speed, speed and more speed, he has very little endurance, he stays in front until he runs out of speed. When he does the 100 metre man takes over, for the 100 metre man relies exclusively on endurance in those last vital 25 metres.

Most coaches are of the opinion that because the 200-metre record is now approaching 1 minute fifty seconds and the 400-metre mark is nearing 3 minutes fifty seconds, these events should almost be classified as sprints. Nothing could be further from the truth. As far as I am concerned, only the 25-metre dash (10 seconds) and the 50-metre sprint (23 seconds) should be truly classified as sprinting. *Sprinting should be based on physiological reasoning, not on empirical standards, convenient man-made distances or an imitation of the athletic programme.* Physiologically the 100 metres is a middle distance event, that must be attacked psychologically as a true sprint. From my way of thinking, the only true sprint is when *maximum* speed is continuously maintained without fade. The track star racing over 100 yards in 9 seconds is truly sprinting; he is exerting maximum pressure all the way without fade.

Sprinting needs a big lift, technically, but especially at administration level. To attract bumper crowds, to bring zest back into swim meets like there was at Concord, U.S.A., to have television companies fighting for the rights to cover the meet, let us have some bright entrepreneur introduce sixty minute super sprint spectaculars. How utterly fantastic to see twenty or so sprints heats each over 25 metres. Pools from necessity, would have to be wider than normal, perhaps 10 or 12 lanes. Each heat would be over in 10 seconds. Electronic timers would decree the fastest times. Computers would spit out the starters for the four quarter finals and then after eliminations the never to be forgotten sight of the twelve finalists crashing to the end within thousandths of a second of each other.

This would be pure sprinting, no need for endurance here except perhaps for breath-holding and nerves. All the strokes and team events could be made up of 25 or 50 metres. There could even be an endurance event of 100 metres. Take the boredom out of present day long meets, keep the older sprinters in the sport longer, create a national super sprint record list and give the spectators something for their dollars besides sore backsides. The big fringe benefit would be that if this type of meet was introduced seriously and nationally for the older sprinters, the listed world records for the long course sprints would all crumble within 12 months. Sprinters and coaches would start to realise what speed was all about. The above is a definite need for sprinters, for we are fast approaching that point where records are starting to last just a little too long. Now let us analyse sprinters and some of their requirements.

Olympic sprint gold medallists, Spitz, Schollander, Wenden, Fraser, to cite a few, had world class times or records over the middle distance to their credit before they won the 100 metres title. I will not elaborate on their schedules but they all had solid distance grounding for many years in their formative stage. All came from camps that worked hard and long. They were the 100 metres sprinters (endurance) types and not the super sprinters (speed) types. Their formative matrix of endurance stood by them in their Olympic year. Clark, Edgar, Austin, Zorn, great super sprint men did not have long-distance orientated backgrounds. All approached or bettered the world sprint records but they could not manage an individual Olympic sprint title.

Of course it all depends what you are seeking. Both targets are a one in a million proposition but world records are easier to achieve than Olympic titles. A super sprinter may have half a dozen chances each year to break the record; for example, a solo swim, a straight-out final or perhaps the lead off in a relay. There will not be as much physical or mental endurance needed as that required by the Olympic finalist who will have to fight his way through heats, semi-finals and finals in two days of fierce international competition, usually in a strange environment in a foreign land. Olympians get their chance only once every four years. *The winners are usually those who have made the best use of the four year term with sprint-type schedules that have some overtones of endurance.*

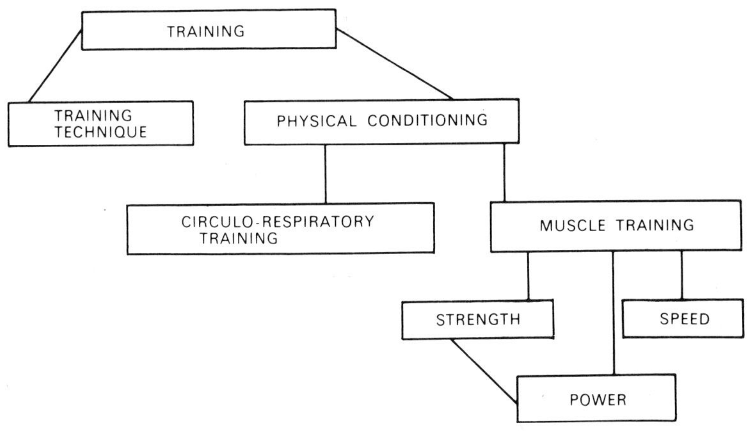

Sprinters need power endurance. Power endurance may be defined as the rate of doing work continuously. Strength plus speed equals power. *We have not as yet reached that point in the conditioning of the mind and body where we are able to exert maximum effort and optimum force on each and every stroke and kick for the entire* 100 *metres.* If we do so, then we would have truly reached the peak of power endurance. Every coach knows that he cannot instruct his charge to go absolutely flat out for the entire 100 metres distance. By flat out I mean the acceleration that one uses when going across the pool in an all-out sprint. It just cannot be done and every sprinter knows it just cannot be done—yet. In across-the-pool sprints we are probably approaching the top strata in power endurance—we can hold all-out speed without fade. Obviously, the longer we can maintain the power endurance or the more equitable we can distribute it throughout the race, the better our personal performance will be. Of course as you mature, year by year, the more efficient your power endurance should become. Peak power endurance is the combination of supreme physical power coupled into the ultimate in determination. Rarely, if ever, does one find a pupil with these dual qualities fully or equally developed. Perhaps it is the hope that one such pupil will emerge, that drives many coaches on, but from historical observations it appears that pupils with superior power endurance emerge from the millions of swimmers about once or twice a decade. We usually designate them as stars "well ahead of their time". The fall off in power endurance is very marked but now with computers to help the mathematical assessment, it is very predictable. This is why it becomes relatively easy to predict the ultimate times that sprinters will achieve over the short distances.

As I write the world record for 100 metres freestyle is 49·99 seconds for men. The world's best sprinters are just on, or just under, 23 seconds for 50 metres and the best "push-off" times recorded for 25 metres are on 11 seconds. On feasible reckoning it is apparent that no one will ever swim 100 metres in 4 times 11 seconds—44 seconds; but it is just within the realms of possibility that some one will swim 2 times 23 seconds—46 seconds, for the long course. And if it is just possible then it will be so. So if the stroke stays the same as it is now, the world record should eventually get down between 44 and 46 seconds for men, and within the range of 50 to 52 seconds for the girls. After all, the men's 100 yards track record has not moved for 12 years and the women's for 16 years, so progression from this point on is going to be painfully slow. Power endurance can be aided by exercises involving equipment or by free exercises using parts of the body as resistance. Most world class sprinters incorporate power building exercises of one form or another in the annual build-up. Iso-gyms, dialex, power rubbers, resistance cords, heavy bar bells are just a few of the aids called upon to help increase or maintain power endurance.

Sprint training is not just repeating fast laps; it is combination of speed and power types of swimming. Tying the feet, pulling a float or resistance, pushing a "loaded" kick board, sprinting in a harness are all beneficial ways of balancing the schedule and building up power endurance.

Ample fatigue endurance is needed to sprint the full 100 metres. It is a chemical situation. The body's capacity to dissipate waste gases and slowing work by-products, its potential to buffer spiralling acid levels, to tolerate the rising oxygen debt or to maintain a steady blood-sugar line, is, as a rule, out of our control. Diet and training can only marginally improve these chemicals situations in our favour. The sprinter fortunate enough to be born with natural assets capable of holding at bay these fatiguing agents a little longer than those of his opponents, has a decided advantage. This section has hardly been investigated and is wide open for researchers. European and Russian physiologists are now intensely pursuing this line of investigation, seeking the magic panacea that will allay fatigue.

There are several ways to delay the onset of fatigue. Fatigue is greatly accelerated by a low haemoglobin level. The lower the level the quicker fatigue appears and the longer it stays. The best chances of a fine performance comes from pupils with normal or higher than normal levels, although it is by no means conclusive for very short sprints.

Oxygen is necessary for efforts so it is essential that the oxygen-carrying capacity of the red blood cells is at its greatest, and secondly, that the number of red cells circulating in the system is at its peak. The intake of first class protein and offal meats, yeast, grain and shell fish with high iron content, is the best natural way to assist the body to increase the haemoglobin in starved red blood cells. Medically, one may assist by the intake of iron tablets either orally or by injection. The oral intake of gradually diffusing iron tablets is one way to try and absorb the mineral, but the danger lies in the fact that the gut may not be receptive to the absorbtion of the iron, so very little enters the blood stream. Injection of iron, or of iron and vitamin B complex together, is accepted as being a more reliable way of getting iron to the blood cells.

The human body is loth to increase the number of red cells within the circulatory system without good cause; when it does so it does it very gradually. Red blood cells are produced in the main from the red bone marrow, especially of the long bones, their release is triggered by the presence of iron-deficient blood cells circulating in the bone area. Once the new blood cells are released and the count goes up the red blood cell factory closes down production. Whilst the new level is usually adequate for normal every day living it may not be high enough for outstanding athletic performance. From my observations, readings below 12·8 grammes for girls and 13·5 grammes for boys over the age of 14 years portends loss of training endurance, poor racing performances and is often the forerunner of illness if hard training is continued. As pointed out, once the level is down it is a long and hard process to lift it. Not enough attention is taken of this critical indicator by some coaches who push for an exhaustive mileage load week after week. Rest, and this means more sleeping hours in bed, restricting training sessions to lighter work or even quitting the pool altogether for a while, will often help the red blood cells to find their natural balance again.

Blood transfusions are one way to lift the cell count. This system has been used often but I have never managed to see any conclusive results. Blood doping is the latest system to receive attention in this area. Swedish researchers may now have developed a technique that is a safe and drug-less way to increase performances. Dr. Bjorn Ekblom of Stockholm's Institute of Sport gave physical education students transfusions of their own red blood cells allowing more oxygen to be carried to the muscles and organs. Ekblom's method is based on a well-established physiological fact; muscles under stress need more oxygen than those that are not. Athletes' muscles soon become fatigued when they are starved of oxygen. To overcome this hunger Ekblom first removed a total of 1200cc of blood from each of the students in three separate bleedings four days apart, then kept the blood in cold storage. The bleedings temporarily reduced the subjects' red cell count and consequently their endurance by about 30 per cent. But the bodies soon replaced the lost blood: 32 days after the initial bleeding Ekblom took the red cells, which had been separated from the blood, and re-infused them into the subjects. The result was a marked increase in the red cell count and an increase of 25 per cent in endurance on treadmill running. Because the body quickly passes off excess red cells the pick up was not permanent. Within 14 days of the infusions the students' performances returned to pre-bleeding levels.

So far no adverse side effects have been noted, but doctors warn that more study is needed to determine if any risk is involved. The Russian coaches are reported to be employing such techniques and a number of U.S. coaches have expressed interest. It is doubtful if the scheme would materially assist sprinters to better performances, but it could possibly be used as an insurance when a sprinter's blood cell count fell low and he needed a lift. Its legality has yet to be challenged and determined, but to my way of thinking it is probably akin to drinking coffee as a stimulating drug before an event. It is a drug in universal use and is therefore acceptable by most.

A careful coach will ensure that his pupils do not reach this stage. If such drastic treatment has to be taken the swimmer sinks into a deep psychological trough, he feels he is washed out, and that he is recuperating whilst his team mates are out in the pool doing valuable training. Stocks falls sharply when a doctor has to be called or training has to be cut back. I cannot stress too strongly that all advice and treatments connected with this critical area of maintaining or lifting the haemoglobin level or the red cell count, from tablet-taking to injections or transfusions must be done through your sports medicine doctor with the full knowledge of your coach and parents.

Fatigue endurance can be minimally improved by the ingestion of certain sugars. In error is the sprinter who consumes copious amounts of glucose or honey just before the event. In my opinion, it is far more important to ensure that the blood sugar level is high for training workouts when the system is subjected to continued stress and the burning-up of sugar; for it is well known, researched and proven that performance falls as the blood sugar drops. It is not likely to drop in a 100 metres sprint unless you are starving before you race, but it will drop in a very hard or prolonged training session. The body has a reservoir of sugar in the liver. When the sugar level drops below the base of the normal range, 72 mg. per ml. of blood for the adult sprinter, adrenalin is pumped into the system from the suprarenal glands, situated above the kidneys. The adrenalin acts as a catalyst on the chemistry within the liver and the sugar is released into the blood stream, thereby maintaining the correct level. The muscles are also minor storerooms of sugar. Sprinters need sugar but not in excess. Pure fruit sugars appear to enter the system faster than do cane or beet sugars, and if sugar is necessary, they are recommended.

In swimming countries with high living standards, United States, Canada, Britain, most of Europe and Australia, the practice of vitamin supplementation has steadied down to a sensible level. Most athletes who do take extra vitamins today do so as a precautionary measure and coaches who prescribe them do so for psychological as well as nutritive reasons. One must admit that there is strong evidence (for people who care about their diet) to recommend the foods that nature provided and, as far as practical, their consumption in a natural state. There are over 200 artificial colourings, additives, preservatives and flavourings registered in Canada. The situation is getting out of hand. Natural flavours, colourings, etc., are being processed out of foods and these are being replaced by synthetic counterparts. It is up to the conscientious coach to organise a natural training table in the homes of his pupils. There is an undeniable link between nutrition, fatigue and endurance. The last fifty years have seen the biggest ever change in man's dietary pattern. Man has suckled nature since before the Mesolithic age, 10,000 years ago. His system has become, for the most part, sympathetic with the gifts that nature provides. Now in the short span of a few decades, science has decided to invade the system with man-made synthetics that the body has not had time, or does not, adapt to. Because of this processing there is support for certain vitamins to be considered in the sprinter's diet. I will now elaborate on a few of the "fashionable" swimming vitamins.

Vitamin C, since it cannot be stored in the body, and since it is partly destroyed by handling, storing and cooking, could be a worthwhile additive to the diet. Recent evidence has shown that gigantic doses of this vitamin may have some harmful side effects, so as in all things, moderation is better, nature is best. Since Vitamin C promotes well-being to muscle and connective tissues its deficiency should be avoided; 200 mg. per day would be a normal intake for the sprinter in training. This would be covered naturally if fruits, particularly citrus, fresh green-leafed vegetables or berries are eaten daily. During conditions of extreme swimming stress all the water-soluble vitamins, as well as vitamin A, are required in larger than normal quantities. This is particularly so with vitamin C which, when under stress conditions, completely disappears from the suprarenals and the serum level falls markedly. Coaches know that by giving their sprinters larger doses of vitamin C, muscular soreness after intense training or racing is reduced rapidly. Vitamin C deficiency signs are tiredness, decreased efficiency, and susceptibility to infections especially those of the respiratory tract. Olympic sprinters in hard training have taken as much as 1,000 mg. per day as a supplementary safeguard, but 200 mg should suffice any training need.

Vitamin B12 is found mostly in first class protein meats, liver and kidneys. It is also in the gut. This vitamin is the factor that triggers off a system for the production of red blood cells and therefore it is vital. It can play an important role in elevating low blood counts. Leading Australian coaches suggest that their swimmers take vitamin B12 tablets during the hard training months or when approaching race time. The dosage varies between 10 and 25 microgrammes daily. As a precautionary measure my sprinters who have low blood counts and who are approaching the national titles, have two or three injections of B12 (each a week apart).

This usually coincides with the commencement of the taper down period for their biggest races of the season. The injections are usually between 250 and 500 microgrammes. I find that the B12 injection, coupled with the ease back in training and more hours of rest, often lifts the haemoglobin appreciably. Recent Olympic finalists who had four injections of vitamin B12 in a period of six weeks, improved their haemoglobin levels significantly. For example, 15·1 to 16·0, 14·5 to 16·2, 14·8 to 16·8, 14·5 to 15·5 for the boys and from 13·7 to 13·8, 15·4 to 15·5, 14·2 to 15·2 and 14·5 to 15·8 for the girls. I do not advocate that a higher than normal haemoglobin level is necessary for everyday training, but it appears that it could be beneficial in those vital last weeks.

The latest nutritional discovery for sport which could be of value to sprinters is vitamin B15. It has three major properties: it assists in the metabolism of fats so that they can be actually used by the body for work; it assists in the utilisation of oxygen by the tissues; and it destroys poisonous substances introduced into the body. Vitamin B15 has a general tonic effect, assisting in sleeping and eating. Although new in the athletic scene, tests with B15 have been very encouraging. Muscular strength and endurance have both been improved in laboratory animal tests. Athletes in heavy work have responded with greater work output and longer endurance even with minute doses of 15 microgrammes daily for three days, the effects lasting for up to three days. Vitamin B15 is found in such things as bran, rice, rice sprouts and ox blood. There are no recognisable symptoms of B15 deficiency and there are no signs of side effects from its use. The Soviet Union is leading the research in this vitamin which has shown remarkable promise in the treatment of cardio-vascular diseases. One of the most important properties of vitamin B15 is that it has a detoxicating action that can eliminate the effects of alcohol and other drugs from the system. From the swimmers' point of view its value and promise lies in the areas of increased endurance without side effects, the increased use of oxygen by the muscles and therefore a delay in the onset of fatigue and the reported increase in strength.

The controversy on the merits or doubtful benefits of vitamin E still rages. Australia has been the leader in the field of vitamin E supplementation for swimmers since 1955. In Australia most coaches still advocate it. Vitamin E is found naturally in vegetables, vegetable oils, grains, liver and meat. Wheat germ oil is the richest source. The advocates of the use of this vitamin insist that it does improve endurance and that it assists in the oxygen capacity of the tissues. The greatest team of sprinters that Australia has ever produced, (Melbourne Olympics 1956, when we filled all three places in the men's and women's sprints and won the sprint relays) were all on large doses of wheat germ oil. The average intake for boys was 1400 mg. per day and for the girls 1000 mg. This fine sprint result underscored the value of vitamin E in the minds of many coaches. Apparently this vitamin assists best when taken in large doses, minor amounts being of little consequence.

Vitamin E is an extraordinary vitamin, needed by every cell in the body and consequently affecting every organ in the body. It is this very versatility that has delayed its full acceptance. Vitamin E is becoming increasingly harder to obtain from our everyday foodstuffs. It is estimated that people at the turn of the century received 15 times more vitamin E from natural sources than we do now. It is also significant that after the turn of this century, when flour became so highly refined and bleached and all the vitamin E was removed, coronary thrombosis became a recognisable disease. Vitamin E is an anti-oxidant. It hinders the too-rapid oxidisation of fats in the cells. It enables them to utilise fats in the proper way. The vitamin is also necessary for the formation of the centre of the nucleus of the cells. It strengthens muscles and promotes the use of proteins and other vitamins in the system, especially vitamin A, thus improving digestion and nutrition. Apparently large doses of vitamin E increase the staying power of horses and greyhounds and I have seen some very convincing literature on experimentation with rats and their subsequent increase of endurance. However, there is not a lot of work issuing from research centres on its effect on endurance in man. It is a safe vitamin to take in supplementary doses but apparently some sprinters have reported a little diarrhoea and a few skin rashes from very heavy dosage.

For girls who may be taking oestrogen for the control of their periodic menstrual cycle and for those on iron tablets there must be a time lapse of 8 to 12 hours between the taking of these and vitamin E, for they are antagonistic to each other. This is why you will have to be careful in working out your tablet schedule if your are ingesting the slowly-diffusing iron tablets. As vitamin E is a fat-soluble vitamin it is not absorbed into the digestive tract unless there is bile present, and supplementary doses should be taken after a meal which contains some oil or fat. Wheat germ, wheat germ oil and cold-pressed vegetable oils, particularly soybean oil, are the richest sources of vitamin E. Next comes wholemeal flour and wholegrain cereals. There is some in butter, margarine made from vegetable oils, liver, kidneys, fish and oysters. Fruits and vegetables have a little. Care should be taken when purchasing tablets to obtain the natural vitamin E capsules, as there are low quality synthetic tablets available.

In summary, most of the world's leading coaches advise the taking of vitamins and minerals in tablet form as a safeguard against deficiencies. One may easily get on the merry-go-round of taking handfuls of tablets daily because this or that is supposed the magic panacea. Sensible coaches suggest one only multi-vitamin and mineral capsule daily. Your sports medicine doctor will advise if extra iron or vitamins would be of benefit to you.

Pain endurance is, for the main part, mental. Some sprinters have a greater pain tolerance than others. Some can resist pain in hard training whilst others succumb to it by reducing the pressure of their work and easing back out of the pain zone. Fortunately in sprinting the pain crescendo peaks mainly in the final stages of the 100 metres sprint and with patience and practice you can educate your mind to accept new thresholds or plateaus of pain. This particular type of endurance is really the ability and the desire of the speeding competitor to maintain or increase his work load in spite of the build-up of physical and mental discomfort. The more it hurts, the harder he tries. This endurance is not measurable, it is an intangible. It is the factor that separates the trier from the quitter. Training pain should be created in gradually increasing doses by the intelligent coach and accepted by the pupil. It is a very personal thing and it places the coach on his mettle to know just how far to push the sprinter. Obviously, if the sprinter can punish himself by heavy and prolonged pain stints in training when there is not much motivation to do so, he will endure more in a race. He is not only doing better quality workouts but he is mentally adjusting himself to the pain necessary for success.

The "hurt, pain, agony" teachings of Doctor James Counsilman call for grit and willpower. Without it you cannot hope for success today. You should expose yourself to increasing doses of training pain, you will survive, nature makes sure of that. It is well known that persons suffering pain from illness, operations or torture can, if the doses are increased gradually and regularly, build up much tolerance and resignation. Pain endurance depends on the power of the mind, and since pain in sprinting is so short-lived, it is a matter of how mentally tough you are and just how great your need to succeed. Let's face it, sprinters have it easy with pain factors in racing, no long merciless grind such as the 1500 metre men endure and that is why the quality of the sprinter's pain has to be greater. Greater in training, greater in performance.

Nervous endurance is the ability of the trainee or the competitor to maintain emotional stability especially when the mental pressure is on in the days prior to competition and during the meet. To be able to sleep soundly on the eve of the race, to take a cool and philosophical outlook on the outcome, can prevent the competitor from mounting the starting blocks half washed out, mentally. If your bank of nervous energy is drawn upon too heavily by anxiety, or depleted by worry, long nights with broken sleep, then a decline in performance is axiomatic. Errors in judgement, loss of confidence, short temper and even physical upsets in digestion are common bed-fellows when the nervous batteries are low. Nervous energy can be likened to a battery, when fully charged by adequate sleep, proper diet and mental tranquility your physical effort will be instantaneous, your output will be strong from brain to nerve endings, you will have "sparkle". If the battery has been sapped by sleep loss or other damaging features, and one of these can be guilt over poor personal effort in training, then your physical energy is below par. Tablets can be prescribed by the doctor for those who have worrying sleepless nights. The tablets that work immediately but wear off within an hour or two, thereby leaving the swimmer asleep naturally, are the best. Sports medicine doctors will instruct their charges to have a trial run with sleeping tablets weeks before the event to detect if there are any side effects or if the pupil's work output is impaired in any way.

A confidence-building talk by the sympathetic coach can work wonders on an anxious charge, for if there is one time when the coach and pupil should draw very close together it is certainly the weeks and days leading up to the big meet. The worth of these chats depends entirely on the ability of the coach to relieve pressure and build confidence, and it is an art that improves with practice. I place tremendous importance on this final talk down, so I often record race instructions and ego-building gospel on tape for the pupil to play back in the privacy of his home, usually on the eve of a race. It is a very individual thing and one can well imagine, ties very strong bonds between pupil and coach. Nerve tonics, usually with the important nerve vitamin B2 added, may help fractionally. Cat naps between sessions will assist in restoring ragged nervous endurance. Novices may find it difficult to sleep in the daytime but by continually trying the living pattern is gradually changed and sleep will come, and once established, is eagerly looked for each day. All international competitors sleep during the day when approaching their titles. Naps vary from 30 minutes to 2 hours and the benefit from these sleeps is usually manifested in a good training session that afternoon. Illness and infection, sore ears, infected sinuses and colds can seriously deplete the nervous bank's credit. If reserves of nervous energy fall too low the pupil becomes disinterested in training sessions, starts to find fault with his coach, the system or his training friends. Girls often sulk or cry, parents become disenchanted, not realising that the situation has been caused initially by a degree of nervous breakdown. The alert coach will not allow this situation to arise. In particular be on guard for:

* irritability, "talking back" to the coach, depression, tears
* general lassitude, frequent yawning, repeatedly arriving late for workouts, skin eruptions, pouches under the eyes, rashes
* swollen or tender lymph glands
* blocked nostrils, sore ears, rhinitis, constant spitting from sinus seepage
* loss of appetite, stomach upsets, swollen liver
* sudden body weight loss, muscle soreness, shortness of breath
* inability to hold "repeat" sprint times
* very high and continually high early morning heart rates, slow recovery rates after effort.

The sprint machine relies on nervous endurance. His zip, his bounce, his sparkle, are dependent on fully-charged batteries; these only come from good health, being happy, adequate rest and diet.

Rhythmic endurance is needed to hold your best form, balance and timing when the stroke is under pressure in hard sprint training or competition. To maintain perfect "form" for the entire distance is the objective. Young or inexperienced sprinters often "go to pieces" during the concluding stages of a hard race. This is the loss of rhythmic endurance. A sprinter "out of form", particularly early in the season when unfit, is low in this endurance. Beginners have none at all. Rhythmic endurance is a taught thing that the body's nervous pathways adapt to and control. It can be improved gradually under the watchful eye of the coach, if the pupil is receptive. There are many methods of teaching it and the intelligent mentor will devise a system to suit his circumstances. Here is the method I employ. The student performs a series of sprints across the pool, the sprints becoming progressively faster. The coach observes the pupil from two poolside positions, preferably one below and one above the water. He assesses and records the pupil's score, keeping mindful of the fact that when marking, *the stroke is a personalised thing which is an individual style within a very narrow range of accepted technical variations, and no two sprinters execute their stroking in a like manner.*

Once the coach and pupil are satisfied with the rhythmic endurance across the pool, that the stroke has held together technically under full pressure, then the series is repeated over the full fifty metres course. The side benefit of this exercise is that the sprinter is impressed by the importance of marrying stroke with speed. Anything less than a 100 per cent effort in the final few sprints tend to invalidate the experiment. Once the young sprinter has mastered the basics and has them adjusted marginally to suit his strength and physique, if this is necessary, then he and the coach can get down to the serious business of perfecting the rhythmic endurance over the 100 metres. Boxers and tennis players often provide a good example of "falling to pieces", "losing touch"; this is a breakdown in rhythmic endurance and it is always associated with poor coaching, fatigue or loss of confidence.

I recall clearly a world record by a former pupil, Olympic sprint champion Jon Henricks. When questioned after a 100 metres event, Jon said that he was sure he would win so he decided to concentrate on technique *for the entire race.* He was amazed at how quickly the finishing wall came up and also at his time. Coaches have known for a long time that if you can get the sprinter to concentrate on style, and let's face it, the sprinter has to do it all his swimming life, his mind is diverted away from the pain and distance. Shortening of the stroke, sloppy entry, lifting the head, pulling wide, breathing too early, dropping the hips, or rolling excessively are only a few indicators of sprinting inadequacy caused by loss of rhythm.

How do you rate as a potential sprint champion on the check list below? Do not be disheartened if you fall short on a few points. There is no one who would score full marks. The list is not complete.

* Are you of European descent? Asiatic, Oriental or Negroid swimmers do not figure prominently in Olympic finals. This could be because these races are not exposed to swimming training as we are. The physiology of the European aligns well with speed requirements in the water. His living standard also helps.

* Were your parents or grandparents prominent athletically, not necessarily in swimming? Having adventurous and vigorous forbears is often an advantage in the quality of tissue and determination.
* Are you strong? Remember, a weak sprinter can look good in the water but cannot endure. This is one facet that you can do something about.
* Are you endowed with a wiry musculature and yet overriding it all is a smooth contour?
* Have you a full-range flexibility? Sprinters need loose shoulders, thin and flexible ankles, a good to excellent range of flexibility in the spine, elbows and knees. The head must have free mobility.
* Have you large hands and feet? The efficiency of man in water is very poor. The larger the hands and feet with the accompanying power to use them, the faster you will be. Whether you use a regular six beat kick or not, small feet hinder progress, large feet assist.
* Do you possess above average co-ordination, sense of balance and rhythm? These qualities can be improved by practice, but the sprinter who possesses these naturally cannot be overtaken in this field.
* Have you a smooth skin? A natural asset the worth of which cannot be disputed or measured. Subjected to harsh water immersion for many hours a day and long spells of sunshine and wind, the swimmer's skin will harden. However, some sprinters possess and retain smooth skin. Physiologists suggest that this asset could help in the sensitive "feel" of the water.
* Are you the correct body weight? If not, then do something about it—gradually.
* Are you taller than average? We are in the era of the six-footers. To be tall and have all the other necessary ingredients of a sprinter places you way out in front, especially in short course.
* Do you float? This is more of an essential for a distance man, but it has benefits for the sprinter in higher flotation and the fact that all his energy can be channelled into forward progression and not a part of it in trying to keep afloat.
* Have you a normal or high haemoglobin level? If so, you have an advantage because your blood stream can absorb more oxygen. There is controversy now as to whether or not the lack of oxygen is the controlling factor in the sprinter's fade. A low haemoglobin level can denote fatigue or stress.
* Have you a large vital capacity? This can be increased by training but the super stars have larger than normal capacities to start with.
* Is your early morning heart rate low? If it is low naturally it could tie up with herity. Distance swimmers, because of the

nature of their continual and repetitive movements, condition the heart rate to function efficiently in the lowest ranges. The sprinter's heart rate at rest can be higher, but certainly lower than the untrained.

* Do you possess the "endurances" outlined in this chapter? Do you possess them in larger-than-life quantities?
* Are you naturally fast in thought, actions, repartee?
* Have you a good health record, free from sinus trouble, 'swimmers' ears', influenza, chronic muscle ailments?
* Do you eat well? Mainly first class proteins and fresh vegetables, fruit and natural foods?
* Do you sleep a minimum of eight hours per day? Do you revitalise your batteries with naps during the day?
* Is there a team doctor or sports medicine doctor available to you, one who appreciates the physical and mental ailments associated with swimming?
* Are you above average in school marks?
* Are you really confident in everyday living and in your swimming or do you just pretend to be?
* Are you a high school or university student?
* Have you all-the-year-round pool and gymnasium facilities available?
* Are you the member of a successful, hard-working team, one that has ambition, prestige, motivation? The best sprinters in the land come from top teams. They never succeed working or competing as 'loners'.
* Have you a top coach, or at least an enthusiastic coach who specializes in sprinters? Because of the college, state and national programmes coaches, from necessity, have to be "Jacks" of all trades. However some coaches have much more success with distance swimmers, others prefer winning with speed men.
* If you are a girl, is the team led by strong sprint males? Do the girls mix in with the boys in sprint training. Australia's best girl sprinters have all come from mixed teams where they have had to swim hard after faster boys.
* No one can possibly work at full pressure all the time, but when you leave the pool after a workout are you completely satisfied with your training?
* Do you and your coach understand each other? Are you working for a target together? Do you communicate freely?
* When you do your sprints are they in the pain zone or the comfort zone?
* Do you do your strengthening exercises daily or at least five times a week with or without equipment?
* Are you regular at training? Ten sessions or more weekly? Do you work between 6000 and 8000 metres per session?

* Do you look forward to training sessions, not only the companionship, etc., but the work as well?
* How many years have you been training? You realise that a minimum of five years is required before you start to make a big impression.
* Do you get encouragement and co-operation from parents, teachers and officials; coach.
* How does your stroke measure up technically? How are your turns? Your starts? Your finishes? Have you weakness in your stroke that is constant? Are you and the coach working on it?
* Is your kick effective as a propelling agent or do you just keep it out of the way? Remember, the very best sprinters have all been six beat kick exponents.
* Have you adequate finance to cater for your equipment, tablets, fees, travel.
* Do you have available transport?
* Does your time improve dramatically in a race? Do you have the "killer" instinct, not only in racing but in training as well?
* Do you abstain from smoking, alcohol, drugs? If not, you might as well resign yourself to the fact that you will never be a top winner.
* Do you play a non-injurious secondary sport, preferably a team sport?
* Is there a superstar blocking your way to the top? If so, are you closing the gap on him? Where does he beat you, on strength, the finish, technique, the turns, his experience, etc.? What are you doing about it?

4. Forming a sprint organisation

Let all things be done decently, and in order.

CORINTHIANS *1, XIV, 40.*

Imagine if you will that we have ample funds, adequate time and the desire to set up the ideal sprint school, and that you are going to be involved. We will take the best features from the best groups, we will draw on experience and we will add worthwhile items of our own. We will keep in mind that although a near perfect plan can be put on paper, it is people within the organisation who decree success or failure. The "complete" swim organisation has yet to be created for it is only since the introduction of the Age Group system in the United States that coaches, parents and swimmers have tried to combine their abilities into a single force, expressed through the local swim club. Prior to this, clubs existed in three separate parts. The best organised groups were the university teams. In Australia there are no well-planned swim clubs combining all the available talents efficiently and pulling in a single direction. Clubs are still developing. Here are the main ingredients for a successful swim structure. Coaches and Swimmers, Facilities, Coaching Organisation.

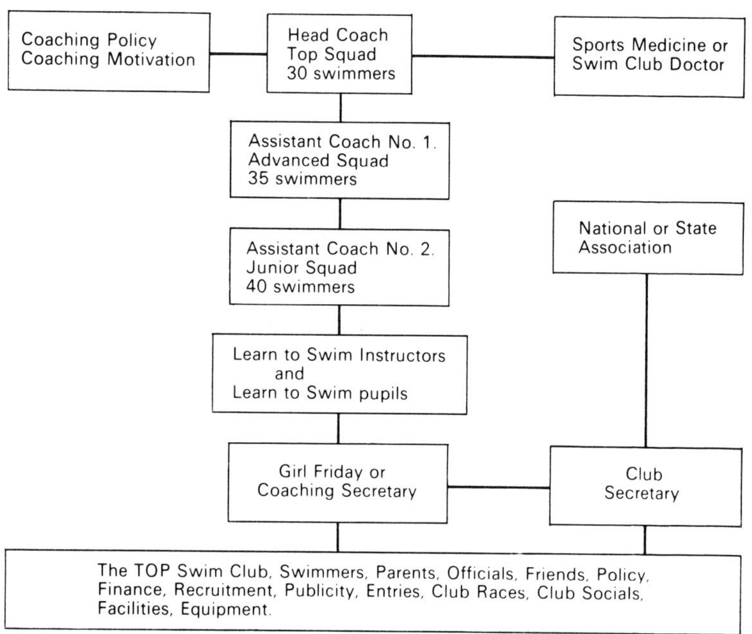

NOTE: Top Squad consists of sprinters who are within 10 seconds of the World record for 100 metres.
Advanced Squad consists of swimmers who are within 20 seconds of the World record for 100 metres.
Junior Squad consists of swimmers who are within 30 seconds of the World record for 100 metres.
(The above standards should be flexible in the early stages of formation).

The Coaches: Their combined talents must include *experience and zest.* The Head Coach must have the ability to organise, he must command respect, have vast sprinting experience not necessarily as a past competitor, a scientific background, the ability to communicate and the desire to succeed. He will be the power house of the unit. His age is not important but he must be old enough confidently to control the older male and female swimmers, some of whom may be in their twenties. He should be mature and successful enough to be professionally admired by his assistant coaches, his staff and the swimmers. He should emanate a feeling of knowledge and solidarity. He should be approachable. He must be a "thinker", prepared to try something new, able to sort the useful from the useless, he must not be tied down by tradition. He should be a reader, for once a coach reaches that stage in his career where he is "too busy" to keep up with the latest written work or where he says to himself "Nothing new here, I tried that years ago", or he fails to keep abreast of the latest ideas, the newest records, the fresh champions, he is declining as a sprint coach. He should be an organised person.

He must have the strength of character to discipline errant pupils, the thoughtfulness to praise the good doers. (George Haines, U.S.A. Olympic coach, once "showed the door" to the world's greatest sprinter, Mark Spitz, for failing to comply with his request). The Coach must have a personal target outside of the fact that he wishes his sprint team to be the greatest. With most coaches it is the honour of being selected as a national coach, the associated travel, usually overseas, and the prestige that success brings. Most top coaches I know seek financial security but they are not money-motivated in preference to doing a good job.

The coach must have ability. Many persons set up as coaches because of the opportunities that fall their way. Some of these people enter the profession for the wrong reasons, many do not have the ability to coach beyond the elementary levels, often they do not have the right knowledge or if they do, they are unable to impart it. They are often lacking in background knowledge of the sciences associated with the sport. Children are demanding swimming attention all over the country, there are not enough coaches to go around, there is room for all within the calling but the coach we are seeking for our super sprint school has to have ability—superior ability. He has to be a Jack Nelson–George Haines–Don Gambril–Jim Montrella–James Counsilman–Peter Daland–Deryk

Snelling–Frank Elm type. In other words, he has to be of a class that can first of all recognise talent or suspect latent ability, and he has to possess all the capabilities to bring the swimmer through to his ultimate best. Some coaches can see the talent in the team but are not sure how to go about developing it, and when they are not sure they often make errors. Others do not see the embryonic champions right under their sunglasses. They do not realise the potential until, in some cases, the sprinter transfers to another team and he starts to progress.

The coach must be impartial, no playing favourites. The truly great youth leader can spread the mantle of his personality over the whole team from the novice to the superstar, and he will be liked by all. Everyone on the team is his "very special sprinter". It may only be a wink or a nod, a hand on the shoulder, a word or two or perhaps a feeling but *you* know you are coach's special sprinter. You do not expect him to show it in front of the team but you *know* you're really number one. Counsilman's fine coaching and handling of those magnificent Indiana teams in winning six consecutive N.C.A.A. finals epitomises the d'Artagnan concept of welding like people together amicably—"all for one and one for all'—and I am *the* one.

The coach must be diplomatic, able to handle the every day problems of the swimmers and the parents with firmness and fairness, able to keep everyone "on side". He must be the suprème prestidigitator. His policy must be logical, based on commonsense and clearly outlined at the beginning of operations. It should be accepted by all and he must adhere to the terms that he has set out, even though at later times, it goes against his own grain to uphold some rulings. "Do not forget promises to pupils", should be one of his own rules, children are still sensitive to such things, and since we are seeking to build a two-way bond of confidence (coach and pupil), the promises cannot be one-sided.

Up-to-date swim schools require either two coaches or one coach with adequate professional assistance available. A head coach, an assistant head coach and several junior coaches are required for teams in excess of 100 swimmers. When one coach is tied down with travel or lecture commitments number two coach can take the helm and maintain the continuity and the standard of the system. Continuity is the keynote of today's successful swim teams. For example, we all know what happens to the trainees for the week that the coach is away at the nationals, they stagnate. The addendums to coaching are numerous. If one is to do a first class poolside job he must be free from associated encumbrances. He must have a good foil in the assistant coach and other helpers. The other coaching combination which succeeds is where the professional coach has all the facilities of a university behind him, where he can call on the physics department, the university workshop, the medical college and the physiology professors and such like, for immediate and authentic information or the help that he requires. These two examples apply to the countries of the western world. The communist countries have a more professional approach and their system involves many coaches and assistants.

The assistant coach should be young, eager to learn, and have to some degree, most of the qualities as outlined for the head coach. If the head coach is to be the mental force on the team the assistant coach should be the physical powerhouse about the pool, not just a lackey to the head coach but an individual, fully versed in the programme and prepared to co-operate fully. He must also be diplomatic, on guard to correct misinterpretations. Often swimmers and parents will confuse the issue by saying "coach told me to do it this way and now you are telling me differently". The two coaches must work as one team, after all they are the professionals and should leave no doubt as to their ability and single-mindedness in stroke, the programme and the policy. The junior coach must be given the responsibility of controlling the top team from time to time, taking the teams on tours, organising the workout. He should be loyal to the coach, for if he has a contract to do a job he should do it wholeheartedly, not just going through the motions and perhaps biding his time and waiting for the opportunity to break away on his own. Organisations such as the Santa Clara Swim Club, Cincinnati Marlins, Pine Crest or Lakewood are the best of their style because of cohesion between coaches–organising personnel–swimmers. They are fully dependent upon co-operation up and down all the links of their cabin for success.

The Swimmers: Numerically the top squad should not exceed 30 sprinters if all are to receive the very best attention. Junior coaches can handle up to 40 pupils each because a lot of their work is not as demanding as the top squad. In the United States the average club membership is over 100, in Australia it is under 100, but figures in excess of 100 are required if the club is to be a force, for there has to be a good flow-on from the learn-to-swim sections to the top squad. A major commitment of a swim club is to make children safe in the water and from these swim classes enthusiastic instructors should channel the youngsters up into the speed system. By the time these swimmers move up to the top groups they will have complied with most of the requirements outlined for sprinters elsewhere in this book.

There is more to being a top sprinter than having the proper physique, a top coach and the right training, adequate pools and facilities. I refer to those intangibles in the "quality" of body and mind. The intelligent sprinter with his mind on the job will have to be told only once or twice to comply with a training procedure or a stroke modification. He will be the type who will swim right to the end of each lap, there will be no stopping short and if lead swimmers are in the way he will swim right through to the wall—hard. He will stay off the bottom of the pool, there will be no one-footed pushoffs from the bottom halfway up the pool when the going gets tough. When the programme calls for "tumbles" he will tumble no matter what angle he hits the wall, no matter how many swimmers are packing up on the wall just ahead of him, no matter how depleted he is. His visits to the changeroom will be legitimate calls of nature not just an excuse to get out for a breather. Our true grit sprinter will show leadership qualities. In the temporary absence of the coach he will keep the team working. He will swim "to time", if the coach calls for "twenty-nines" he will do all in his power to stay on target time, not just for the first few but for the whole series. He will pass slower swimmers in his lane without slackening his pace, but he will do it in a workmanlike manner, not with a kick or a shove that will send his team mate to the bottom of the pool. He will not talk much, he will be, for the most part, concentrating, not that he will be a zombie but juvenile talk and behaviour are just not his "cup of tea". He will not waste effort in his rest periods by making water geysers through his front teeth or squirting water jets through his hands, he will be serious but not dull. His attitude to training will influence others to imitate.

Our top boy will have a fair share of water sense, in training and in competition. He will use his lane and his water space intelligently. He will be aware of what the other sprinters in the team are doing but it will not upset him, it will "keep him on the ball". In order to make his training quality a little better than the rest he will, from time to time, capitalise on other members of the team, but he will do it in such a manner that it is not obvious or unsportsmanlike. Of swimmers I have coached, world record holder Brad Cooper, was a fine exponent of this art. He had many tricks up his sleeve, such as swimming his 100 metres repeat sprints without using his legs when all the other swimmers were using theirs. He would come in slightly behind the leading swimmers giving them false hope that he was not going so well. Another psychological plan he often used, was to have a full meal and do a complete weight and pulley workout just prior to the afternoon swim session. He would try hard in training but the sparkle would be gone and his opposition would think he was losing form. Many fine tactical training sessions he had with his team-mate, Stephen Holland, who also was endowed with great water cleverness.

Reliability will be a feature of our sprint star's makeup, he will be punctual and regular for sessions, early for meets. He will carry out his everyday chores, such as home exercises, log book details, packing his gear bag, taking any necessary tablets or perhaps medicating his ears, without constant reminders from his parents and coach. If the coach knows he has a reliable sprinter, in the water and out of it, the pupil becomes almost predictable in training. If he starts to fade a little in his power work or if his output is somehow lacking, the alert coach can detect it almost immediately, a conference is called and the remedy taken. Not so with the wishy-washy trainee whose effort and output varies from session to session, or even sprint to sprint, a coach can never tell when he is "on form" or "off". It is difficult for an enthusiastic coach to remain so with these pupils.

The ideal sprinter will communicate, if there is a lack of dialogue between coach and pupil it is usually the fault of the coach. An international coach with a very large squad admitted to me that he did not talk much to his pupils because he was never sure of some of their names. He knew their form and their stroke but as for the names of the "lesser lights" they were mostly addressed "Hey you!"—hardly the way to gain the pupil's confidence. Nevertheless, the dialogue must flow both ways. Coach's enquiries such as "how does that stroke feel?" or "how hard was that sprint?" require accurate answers. The coach on poolside, as a general rule, does not have time for verbal pleasantries, he seeks a fairly accurate response to his questions for professional reasons. This is why the sprinter must know himself. He must be sensitive to his stroke, his condition, his feel of the water and sundry things, but not over-sensitive, for there are few things worse than the ever-complaining pupil, every minor indisposition real or imaginary being reported in great detail. It becomes a case of the boy who cried wolf, when real problems arise the coach tends to gloss over them. The other end of the scale is the sprinter who feels that it is a weakness to admit to illness or problems and he keeps them to himself. Muscle soreness can turn to a chronic injury, sore ears can precipitate into a serious infection, hidden fears or misunderstandings can coalesce into a mental block, so we need a sprinter who is intelligent, knows when to talk to the coach and the right things to report. Coaches should be on guard to listen to the pupil, not just appear to listen whilst thinking of other things, giving hand signals to other members of the team or breaking across the conversation with instructions to others. The coach must be attentive and responsive to requests, reports and information from pupils. What seems trivial to the coach may be of major proportions to the sprinter. The coach can observe and evaluate most training "signs" but rare indeed is the coach who can assess to the nth degree the pupil's feelings, potential and effort. Intelligent discourse regularly will tend to keep coach and pupil in focus.

The Organisation: A coaching plan based on commonsense is the key to a successful team. Poor organisation negates the good work of individuals in the group, swimmers leave, parents become disgruntled and the team falls lower and lower down the list of top clubs. The success of the organisation in the first instance depends upon the drive and personality of the coach. Once established on a firm basis and with a sound set of principles, the club should be self-perpetuating, going from strength to strength and only requiring an occasional injection from the coach to push it up to new levels and ambitions. Of course, if the group is fortunate enough to have a set of controlling personnel who are officiating to truly help the team and not for personal reasons, then success is automatic. The organisation should be managed from two points, coaching and administration. The coaching organisation is the brain child of the head coach. His ideal plan will encompass all things necessary for the welfare and advancement of his pupils as a speed swimmer and as a person. The coaching plan should cover:

* The quantity of training
* The quality of training
* The best combination of the stroke segments
* The most advantageous way to use the pool
* Poolside motivating systems
* Girl Friday

The Quantity of Work: An essential in any training scheme is the performance of sufficient training. The actual loading depends upon the age of the swimmers, their health, their previous experience, the time and the pool space available, the stage of the swimmers' preparation and their sex. During the early conditioning months, many of the top teams exceed 4,000 metres an hour in endurance-type training, some teams have been as high as 4,500 metres but generally speaking this work is medium in quality and hard to maintain even for distance swimmers, and of course impossible for sprinters. The very highest quality work may be as low as 1,500 metres per hour. When assessing the time economics of the workout one must take into account the total time spent in travelling, changing and training. If it takes three hours from door-to-door and only 2,000 or 3,000 metres are covered in training, then the coach should take a critical look at his schedule, for some replanning is necessary. The time used unwisely in this one session is not so important but if the swimmer, the parent and the transport are all tied up in this uneconomical mode for months or even years, then the system is unrealistic and should be scrapped. Should the weekly mileage be down then the time spent at the pool should be reduced also.

Three of Australia's all time great sprinters, Shane Gould, Dawn Fraser and Michael Wenden, had weekly averages of 30 miles (40 kms.), 20 miles (22 kms.), and 22 miles (35 kms.) during their heaviest training years, which seems to indicate that just under 30 miles (48 kms.) per week may be sufficient work for mature sprinters who specialise in quality. Sonya Gray (58·20, 2:03·70, 4:19·26 long course), the present Australian sprint champion, averages 28 miles (45 kms.) per week. World-wide training loads have now stabilised between 10,000 metres and 18,000 metres daily for the developing swimmers, the sprinters being at the lower end of the scale. Mature sprinters swim from 8,000 to 12,000 metres daily. A good rule-of-thumb guide that has been used over the years is to have the pupil swim 1,000 metres for every year of his age, ten-year-old's would be going 10,000 metres daily gradually reaching to a peak at 16 or 17 years of age. From this point on the work load decreases, for the skill has been mastered, the body's recuperative powers are not so fast and life's demands are assuming more importance. As the work load is reduced the rest intervals and the quality should increase. The thoughtful coach will establish quantity loads for his pupils as *individuals* and not en masse, the total loading being dependent upon the pupils capacity to carry the work, and pool time/space.

Mike Curington (52·70, 1:54·61, long course) U.S.A., swims a typical quantity-quality programme.

Mid-season Long Course, Mornings (metres):

Warm-up: Swim 500 Kick 500

Workout: Swim 1,500–1,000–500–400–300–200–100 freestyle with the effort increasing as the distances decrease, 30 seconds rest intervals.
Swim 10 × 100 on the 1:30 as hard efforts
Swim 20 × 50 butterfly on the minute
Total: 7,000 metres.

Mid-season Short Course, Afternoons (yards):

Warm-up: Swim 500, Kick 500, Pull 500

Workout: Swim 4 sets of 10 × 100 freestyle on the 1:30, 1:20, 1:15 and 1:10
Pull 1,000 for stroke and strength
Swim 10 × 50 butterfly
Total: 7,000 yards.

Quantity in training depends on the long term, one good session now and then forms no background for success. Many continuous weeks of work-loads up to the limit of the pupil's capacity are needed to condition the sprinter. Australian coach Les Lazarus, has trained his star sprinter Sonya Gray, on a carefully graduated long range schedule. He plans for maximum quantity and quality in 1976 for the attack on the Montreal Olympics. Sonya's annual mileage and best times for her ages are:

10 years	100 m. freestyle	1:14·6	497 miles (800 km.)
11 years	100 m. freestyle	1:10·6	621 miles (1000 km.)
12 years	100 m. freestyle	1:04·9	746 miles (1200 km.)
13 years	100 m. freestyle	1:02·1	994 miles (1600 km.)
14 years	100 m. freestyle	58·9	1243 miles (2000 km.)

Sonya started elementary training at the age of seven, a high percentage of her work being short course sprint type.

In analysing Shane Gould's (58·5 2:03·5, 4:19·0 long course) long career we find that a lot of swim-fun time was spent in the water during her happy childhood days, naturally this could not be recorded. Before she was three years she could swim under water, at four she could dog paddle, at five she was swimming and snorkelling around the reefs of the Pacific island of Fiji. When Shane was six, she had her first professional swim lessons but a lot of swimming stamina had already been built into those lithe muscles by running about the island, climbing the palm trees, swimming and playing for countless hours in the tropic waters. Her diet consisted mainly of fresh fruit, fish and meats so one may assume that Shane's childhood was built upon the best exercises for swimming (climbing and swimming) and a healthy environment. Some serious training started from the age of eight and she became reasonably proficient in all strokes except butterfly. At nine years she joined her first squad and started to swim a few miles weekly; she had her initial mini success at this age, gaining a place in the breaststroke state titles of New South Wales for nine-year-old's. From the age of ten we have an accurate record of Shane's mileage. Sixty to seventy per cent of all her work was performed in a 25 metres pool. Shane's annual mileage and best times for the 100 metres for her ages are:

10 years	100 m. freestyle	1:18·3	450 miles (724 km.)
11 years	100 m. freestyle	1:08·3	500 miles (805 km.)
12 years	100 m. freestyle	1:05·7	550 miles (885 km.)
13 years	100 m. freestyle	1:01·9	850 miles (1368 km.)
14 years	100 m. freestyle	58·9	1200 miles (1931 km.)
15 years	100 m. freestyle	58·5	1500 miles (2414 km.)
16 years	100 m. freestyle	58·9	500 miles (805 km.)

Shane Gould must be considered one of the most "complete" swimmers of all time, having held all the freestyle world records from 100 metres to 1,500 metres. She annexed the world mark for the 200 metres medley. The quantity of her work or time in the water over a period of 14 years was considerable, it gave her that rare combination of speed and endurance in almost equal quantities. In quantity terms Shane has probably done more mileage in her long career, in order to capture the world record for the 100 metres, than any other girl sprinter. The uniqueness of her versatility was to some degree, her main problem. At Munich she presented Olympic coach Don Talbot, with an unenviable dilemma—she qualified for thirteen events, and was capable of placing, at least, in all of them. Her entry into the 200 metres individual medley, which she won in world record time, was a last minute decision. It is possible, had the Olympic events been in a different order, that she would have won more than the 3 gold medals. I emphasise this multi-race qualification feat of Shane's to assert my statement that her training mileage in the Olympic year, and the years preceding, was almost the ideal. She was the fittest female swimmer in the Games, and coaches and swimmers could hardly do better than to imitate her mileages.

The girl who has done the least work to become an all-time great sprinter is Dawn Fraser (58·9, 2:11·6 long course). Throughout a long career during the 1950s and 1960s her average daily mileage was less than one mile a day. One must remember however, that back in that period the "season" in Australia was from October to March followed by a long winter break. Her quantity load is worth recording here as a comparison and also as she is considered the most enduring woman sprinter in the history of the sport. Here is her mileage and annual best times for the 100 metres over the last 10 years of her competitive career:

18 years	100 m. freestyle	1:06·1	260 miles (418 km.)
19 years	100 m. freestyle	1:02·0	398 miles (641 km.)
20 years	100 m. freestyle	1:01·6	261 miles (420 km.)
21 years	100 m. freestyle	1:01·6	428 miles (689 km.)
22 years	100 m. freestyle	1:00·2	464 miles (747 km.)
23 years	100 m. freestyle	1:00·4	469 miles (755 km.)
24 years	100 m. freestyle	1:00·3	348 miles (560 km.)
25 years	100 m. freestyle	59·9	444 miles (715 km.)
26 years	100 m. freestyle	1:00·2	303 miles (488 km.)
27 years	100 m. freestyle	58·9	283 miles (455 km.)

At 27 years of age, Dawn weighed 10 stones 8 pounds.

It should be pointed out that Dawn Fraser was disqualified from swimming competitions for ten years at the age of 27. At this point in her career she had no intention of retiring and it is possible that she had many more excellent swims still in her. In an exhibition swim in Mexico City at the age of 31, she swam 50 metres in 28·9 seconds and the 100 metres in 67 seconds, in spite of not having trained for 4 years. The quantity of work the sprinter requires should depend, to a large extent, upon his ability; the greater the ability the less training required. This explains to some degree why Dawn Fraser succeeded on such low mileage, by today's standards. She had unequalled natural speed and although girls' records over 50 metres are not universally recognised, her time of 26·8 seconds for 50 metres long course must be one of the fastest ever recorded. The fact that she made all her records with such ease of stroke proves my point about ability.

This is why sprinters must be treated as individuals, even more so than distance swimmers. The adequately trained, healthy sprinter has an individual limit which must be searched out by the observant coach. To push him past his limit is to court danger. Professor Hans Seyle's prophetic words become very appropriate in the regulating of the stress load for sprinters—"*fight for the highest attainment goal but do not put up continued resistance to stress in vain*".

Mark Spitz trained long and hard before he gained his world sprint records. He was in training at 8 years of age. At the age of 10 he came under the tutelage of coach Sherm Chavoor, a Spartan task-master who prescribed long training programmes, his team was probably the hardest working group in the world at that stage. Mark then spent several years with the world's leading swim club, Santa Clara, most of the time under George Haines, whose training philosophy was geared towards quality sprinting and hard training up to the middle distance. James Counsilman coached Mark for the last part of his career. Counsilman is considered by many as the leading scientific conditioner of today. Mark Spitz was fortunate in having three of the world's leading coaches to guide him through the very heavy work load over a period of fourteen years.

Sprinters as a general rule are not agonists, that is, having the love of long hard, hurting work in training. They accept pain in competition. I believe the coach plays a more important role in the production of sprinters than in other types of swimmers, for although the quantity of work is down the quality is up and often sprinters have to be made to *hurt themselves in training*. Quantity is therefore largely controllable and it is the responsibility of the coach in the first instance, the acceptance by the pupil in the second. The coach's ingenuity and determination decrees the level.

The Quality of the Work: The well-worn adage still applies—"when in doubt it is better to sacrifice quantity for quality". Rare indeed are sprint stars like Frank Elm's Kathy Heddy (57·9 long course) who "works 100 per cent at every practice on every stroke". Quality in the workout is certainly the secret of Kathy Heddy's success. Quality not only refers to the total effort output, it includes excellence in stroking, quality thinking, pressure-packed kick and pull sections, and much more. Like quantity, quality is only worthwhile if practised continually and not haphazardly. The quality of training depends almost upon the quality of the mental approach. To think hard means to train hard, for sprinters and coaches. Australia's decline as a sprint nation has been accelerated by a lack of quality (in preference to quantity), the neglect of the kicking drills and the disregard for the finer technique. Canada and the two Germanys have made spectacular advances recently due mainly to an upgrading of quality coaching.

In terms of effort, my squad training motto of "ninety per cent of all the work to be a ninety per cent effort ninety per cent of the time", is a good yardstick for sprinters. Sprinters should analyse their programmes to see if they are high in quality, remembering that it takes more than hard work in one section to make a worthwhile quality workout. To increase quality many schedules should eliminate slow warm-up swims, go straight into repeat 50 metres sprints or similar, with a gradual increase in effort as the swimmers settle down. Slow kicking as a warm-up is of little use as it often turns into a social swim and is of no benefit either technically or cardiovascularly, besides looking very unprofessional. The effort and quality output is a two way split, the coach should push for it, the pupil should try for it. At least half of all kick and pull sprints should be close to the all-out speed, the balance being only a few per cent slower.

In efforts on the main stroke again fifty per cent of the sprints should approach maximum speed, for example, in repeat 100 metres swims departing every 2 minutes, a "1:10·0 swimmer" would be expected to do 1:13·0 to 1:14·0 from "push" for sixty per cent of the sprints, the balance being only a fraction slower. In a very short series (10 or 5 repeats) the sprints should be the highest quality with the pupil shooting for 1:12·0 to 1:12·5. It will be up to the coach to decide if more rest is needed between the efforts in order to keep the quality high. In a series of sprints across the pool, over 75 per cent should be at maximum speed with perhaps an occasional "breather" taken with a slower one. In most circumstances "walk back" sprints should be eliminated, they are too time consuming. Far better for the coach to walk from end to end as the sprinters sprint, giving them the feeling that he is totally involved as he chats to them about their times, their starts, their stroke. If there is a time for relaxed swimming it should be at the end of the schedule. Ten minutes spent correcting a fault or strengthening a weak section can be incorporated with a cardiovascular cool-down swim.

The East German coaches determine the quality and quantity of the individual swimmer's workout from the results of blood samples taken each day before training commences. The type of work that Kornelia Ender, Rosemarie Kother, Ulrike Richter and their teammates do for the day depends to a large extent on the results that the computers announce from the blood sampling. The team doctors make sure that the individual's output in quality and quantity never exceeds the swimmer's physiological limits. Scientific procedures such as this are usually beyond the scope and facilities of the average squad, especially where large numbers are involved, but there is validity for some research and testing to be carried out once or twice a month on the very advanced sprinters of most teams when the work load is severe.

The East Germans average 12 kilometres a day in the early part of their 330 day training "year", the work quality not being particularly high, attention being given to technique. When the programme moves from the endurance stage to the speed-endurance period and especially into the speed training section (usually the last three months) the quality of their work is excellent. Since the East Germans are, in the main, sprinters their training load of 70 kilometres a week of quality work is comparable to the U.S.A. and Australian sprint schedules. Their present wave of success is due to specialisation (specific sprint training) and individual schedules, the quality of their coaches and the attention of over 100 sports medicine doctors throughout the country, not to mention of course, the national desire to succeed. *They are the best psychologically prepared swimmers competing today.*

Sprinters, when considering the quality of their own work, should look further afield than just their own teammates. If you need an incentive to work well keep mindful of the fact that throughout the country right at this moment there are probably hundreds, if not thousands, of sprinters in your age group pushing out quality work over 50 and 100 metres. Some of these sprinters you will meet one day in competition and the outcome to a large extent depends on the sum total of all your quality work. Your quality has to be the best in the land not just the best in your pool or your area. Coaches should remember when setting those weekly schedules that there are hundreds of very astute professional men working with very smart amateur swimmers aiming for quality perfection.

On special occasions quality par excellence can be achieved by some sprinters over a very short series. If the sprinter knows that maximum output is required for a minimum amount of special sprints he will usually respond favourably. A fine example of quality work was performed recently by Australia's (and perhaps the world's) fastest 12-year-old girl, Lisa Curry. She was talked into a series of five super sprints, departing every three minutes. I timed her at 29·01, 28·86, 29·01, 28·88 and 28·45, all better than her best official time of 29·30. The next week she put up the fastest time in the nation for her age, 28·30 for the 50 metres long course. Quality control is a partnership but it all hinges on one pivot, the pupil's built in "want to". The coach can push out quantity with either willing or unwilling pupils but quality will only come from the eager sprinter who is rarely satisfied with his or her effort.

The Ratio of the Stroke Segments: If we have limited time, if we are seeking quality work, if our stroke is to obtain its greatest potential then we should work out scientifically. In the quest for unreasonable mileage (it did get as high as 83 miles a week at one stage in Australia) kicking practices are often cut back, secondary strokes are cancelled because they are too slow, the pulling sections are curtailed. The sprinter needs a balanced workout. Straight sprinting can be overdone, pulling the tube can be overdone, kicking can be underdone, starts and turns can be underdone, etc. The secret of the complete sprinter is to have every section of his stroke fully conditioned and co-ordinated. Today's accepted sprint schedules run close to these lines:

* Pulling practice 30 per cent
* Kicking practice 20 per cent
* Training over 100 metres distances or longer on freestyle 20 per cent
* Training over 50 metres distances or less on all strokes, but mainly freestyle 20 per cent
* Special needs 10 per cent

There are individual exceptions. Australia's current sprint champion, Sonya Gray, uses hand paddles for sixty per cent of all her work whether it be basic training or sprinting.

Her sectional breakdown is:

* Warm-up 12½ per cent
* Swimming distances beyond 100 metres 25 per cent
* Kick sprints 12½ per cent
* Sprints of 50 metres 37½ per cent
* Sprints below 50 metres 12½ per cent

To avoid monotony the coach should vary the ways of doing each section (and there are hundreds of variations) but basically his programmes must be built upon sound principles.

Sandra Bails (61·8, 2:09·8, 4:27·3 long course), Australian Age Champion, shows signs of developing into a top sprinter. Because she is in the formative stage (13 years) her schedule is tailored to suit her:

* Warm-up, stroke correction and secondary strokes 25 per cent
* Pulling and efforts in excess of 100 metres 25 per cent

* Kicking sprints 12½ per cent
* Sprints of 50 metres or less 37½ per cent

A most unique sprint trainee today is Kathy Heddy. Many of her workouts follow this pattern:

* Swimming all strokes, but mainly distance freestyle 60 per cent
* Kicking practice (100 metres repeats) 10 per cent
* Pulling practice (100 metres repeats) 30 per cent

The use of the stopwatch and the keeping of records are the only ways to determine if the sprinters' various stroke segments are at the top of their condition or not. Dr. Richard Jochums, Long Beach Swim Club, U.S.A., has produced a successful team of fast swimmers by using a schedule that relies heavily on pulling practice. In a schedule of 7,000 metres, his team, which includes Tim Shaw, multiple world record holder, would:

* Kick 20 per cent
* Pull 40 per cent
* Swim 40 per cent

In some workouts the pulling load can go as high as 50 or 60 per cent of the total with the kicking staying at 20 per cent. Jochums insists on intensity in the workouts and although his schedules rarely go beyond 14,000 metres in a day, his three segments, pulling, kicking and the whole stroke are exceptionally high in quality.

A training segment not to be neglected is stroke correction for the group and for the individual. In the mini and elementary squads bulk stroke correction can be undertaken with good results, but with advanced pupils smaller group sessions and individual stroke correction is necessary. I have found the following system highly successful for the juniors:

* The head coach lectures to the group making sure to "talk down" to the mini level of understanding. (It is surprising how many young swimmers do not know the correct meaning of words such as resistance, co-ordinate, extension, and how many have difficulty in differentiating between the left and right arms, or can point to various parts of the body when they are named).
* The head coach now briefly demonstrates, in or out of the water, the evolution of part of a stroke, say, in this instance the kick cycle. He explains how it has become a very essential part of the sprint scene, etc. Photographs or drawings can be shown to advantage.
* He then outlines the exact method that he wants all the squad to learn, pointing out the reasons. He may demonstrate a few negative methods of executing a movement, such as trying to kick freestyle with the toes turned out instead of in. Later he will have the pupils try this to impress them with the validity of his statement that in the freestyle kick the toes should be turned slightly in and not out.
* The squad now breaks down into smaller groups and the assistant

coaches run the teams through the kicking drills. Fifteen minutes can be spent on this section. In the final minutes the head coach calls for a "trial for style"; he selects the most correct swimmers and has them swim a lap of honour demonstrating their technique.

* The head coach now goes through the whole procedure again, this time demonstrating the arm action, with the assistant coaches co-operating as before. In one hour, three twenty minute segments can be covered, arms, legs, breathing, timing, starts, turns, finishes, etc. This has to be an important training feature at least once a week. It is appreciated by parents and swimmers alike for on "stroke night" the numbers in attendance almost double. My staff and I take 12 weeks to cover all aspects of all the strokes and the final outcome of the exercise is to issue a "Certificate of Stroking Excellence" to successful swimmers on examination day. Swimmers may not be upgraded to the next squad unless they have their certificate. As far as I know, we are the only group who emphasise the value of correct fundamentals in such a manner. Individual attention is given to swimmers who are having problems, once a week immediately after club races.

With advanced students the method is different. Once a week before training commences, the top team is assembled and the head coach and the assistant coaches point out all the errors or shortcomings of each swimmer. For example, "John, you know we are trying to get that left hand on to the water before the elbow? Well, you have improved a lot during the week but we have noticed that when you are tiring at the end of the efforts, you are reverting back to your old habit; now here is what I want you to do, etc." We never belittle the sprinter in front of the team. We may only spend a few minutes on each swimmer in this fashion, but it is very personalised, and we do keep continually reminding him throughout the week of his faults. Pupils with good technique are complimented on it and told to try and hold it. Every swimmer gets a mention, be it for praise or correction. The team is told of happenings in other camps in regard to stroke or quality, but in the main the time is taken up with individual stroke correction and general stroke principles. Besides this team effort, each pupil is given individual stroke correction once a week. The assistant coaches put through seven or eight pupils daily and the head coach puts through about five. We can cover over 100 a week on a rotating roster system.

Lakewood's (U.S.A.) head coach, Jim Montrella, has regular "talk-ins" where he reports to the team on the latest happenings in other groups, the latest in technique, the best of the current stories in the swimming magazines. It is a very commendable feature for it makes the swimmers realise that "coach is up with things". Most swim clubs have regular swim film evenings, and it is a good way to teach, but unfortunately the dialogue of many of the films is misleading or out of date and there are not enough good films to adequately cover the sport. We are mostly exposed to the American films and therefore our views are becoming one-sided. It requires a lot of thought and preparation to set up a good training programme. It must not be an idea that the coach concocts whilst driving to the pool of a morning; it has to be set up scientifically on a weekly, monthly and a season basis.

The Best Use of Pool Space: Not many swim teams are fortunate to have ample space available all the time, anyway, I have found that when this is so the team may become complacent and spoilt. The coach must use his space economically, but not in such a restricted way that it prevents the pupil from stroking correctly or from getting a long, clear run in his efforts. The majority of coaches have to use public facilities and the allocation of space depends on the whims of the pool manager or the pool loading by the general public. Sprinters require more clear water space than do distance swimmers because they are moving faster and therefore prone to pool crashes, minor accidents. Secondly, a sprinter put "off balance" in the middle of a sprint by bumping into someone seldom regains his speed or stroking by the end of the lap, and the quality starts to suffer as do the coach's nerves. Here are some ideas in pool space planning:

* In repeat 25 or 50 metres swims (in a 50 metres pool) have half of the swimmers in each lane depart from opposite ends of the pool, so that when sprinting they pass approximately at the half-way mark. This way you can comfortably have as many as twenty sprinters in one fifty metres lane swimming in two single files. This system is only good for 50 or 100 metres work. Select a strong leader for each group. With only ten sprinters or less in each file, the work can be maintained at high quality level and most sprinters can swim right to the wall.
* If your sprinters, because of transport or other reasons, arrive at the pool at staggered times you can occasionally run a circuit in the following manner:
  1. as the swimmer arrives he goes into lane 1 and swims 15 × 100 metres kick sprints departing every 2 minutes;
  2. he then proceeds to lane 2 where he swims 15 × 100 metres pull sprints departing every 1 minute 45 seconds;
  3. he then moves to lane 3 where he swims 15 × 100 metres main stroke departing every 1 minute 30 seconds;
  4. he then goes to lane 4 where he sprints 40 × 50 metres swims departing every 45 seconds. Etc, etc.

  The above circuit can have numerous variations. It is advantageous because the team uses only a minimum of pool space early in the programme, but they gradually spill out into the other lanes as the public leaves the pool (afternoon sessions). No matter what time the swimmer arrives for training he will start at the beginning of the programme, thereby not missing any work and not interfering with other swimmers. Also, in this system the lanes do not become overcrowded because the rest intervals are so designed to prevent this. If gymnasium equipment is to be used at the end of the workout in a similar style of circuit, the handling of equipment is required also.

* When very short work is being done by all the team, lanes 1 and 2 can be used for 25 metres "walk back" sprints (in a 50 metres pool), by some of the team. The other end of the pool can be used for "across the pool sprints" or relays at the same time. Also lanes 6, 7 and 8 can be used for starting and "take over" practice using the starting blocks. If you have sufficient coaches you can also use the area near the 25 metres mark in lanes 7 and 8 for turning practice, using the side wall.
* In very small pools rubber harnesses can be anchored along the wall and sprinters can do a series of fast sprint movements in the harnesses. The other part of the pool can be used simultaneously.
* Schedules can be made, perhaps once or twice a week in the early part of the season, where a circuit using the pool and the gymnasium equally can be employed. The team is split into two groups. Group one uses the pool for twenty minutes while group two uses the gymnasium for a similar time. There are coaches at both points. Every twenty minutes the teams change over. If a gymnasium is not available at pool side the grassed area can be used for land exercises.
* A large amount of high quality sprinting can be achieved by swimming three men in a relay for an hour. With two teams in each 7-feet lane and with 8 lanes, forty–eight sprinters are accommodated at the same time.
* In a pool 25 metres by 50 ft. or so, 36, 39 or 42 sprinters can work at once by relaying across the pool in teams of three. This is particularly good for mini squads who do not take up so much water space. Sprinting from push off is safer and the teams should have a few practice half pace try outs first to orientate the swimmers with their area.

To make the best use of pool space it may be necessary at times to remove lane markers. Do not let your placement of swimmers in the pool cut down on the quality of the programme. Always have the fastest sprinters lead the lanes, or all the top sprinters in one lane. In chain work, five second intervals seems the ideal for swimmers to depart. It allows for clear vision, smooth water, a chance to tumble without interference and the opportunity to try to chase someone faster who is out in front.

Girl Friday: Coaching pool side is high pressure, necessitated from the facts that time is usually limited and that the quantity and quality of the work depends largely upon the physical presence of the active coaches on the deck. To have an assistant capable of intelligently handling the sundry telephone calls, messages and requests that always seem to occur when training is at its heaviest, is indeed a blessing, for it allows the coaches to coach with continuity. To be able to walk on to the training deck knowing that Girl Friday has all the equipment in place, that the clocks are going and that today's schedule is being written on the board, helps to put the coaches in a "let's get going" frame of mind. Of course, there are numerous things she can do, timing and recording upon request, typing, making publicity arrangements, keeping the motivating notice boards "alive", helping sprinters with their race entry forms and much more. Girl Friday must have her own self starter.

There is, however, one major function for our helper. She must act as a buffer between parents and coach. Naturally, important issues must get the attention of the coaches but queries as to lost property, next week's training times, fees, etc., should be adequately handled by her. In a large organisation these trivial things can be too numerous and irritating for the coaches to handle personally. Not that coaches should be aloof from the parents, there should be good rapport. The parents can be of great assistance to the coach.

A system that works well in relieving unnecessary pressure from the coaches at home is the "two phone" plan. The team is instructed that relatively unimportant matters which require attention outside of training hours, will be handled by Girl Friday, on the "Warm Line", her home telephone number. With matters of importance the parents or the pupils must contact the coaches directly on the "Hot Line". When the telephone rings at home (I specify between 7.30 and 8.00 p.m.) the coach knows the matter is urgent, someone has a problem and counselling is required.

The position of coaches' assistant is universally honorary so a good plan is to have a trained stand-by available. Equally meritorious is to have the swim club secretary and the assistant secretary play dual roles as Girls Friday. In a large organisation, however, this is not practical as there is ample work for the club secretaries without doing the chores of Girl Friday.

Poolside Motivating Systems: Here are a few suggestions to inspire the sprinters.

* Install an "Honour board" of all time great team members.
* Install a "Pool Record" board for team members only. Cover all distances from 25 metres on.
* Install an "Achievement" board, the names and placings of swimmers in the team who are listed in the national or state-rating lists to be placed thereon.
* Install a "Roll" board with the names of all team members on it and at the end of each day hang distinctive markers opposite the names of the "sprinters for the day". Elaborate boards have an electric lighting system.
* Install a "Closing the Gap" board on which small markers (metal silhouette of a sprinter) can be pushed along a track and locked into position approximating the sprinter's distance in metres

behind the national record. This system can be very motivating for the relay teams.

* Install a 3 column "Seed" board. The headings of the three columns to be:

Sprinters within 5 seconds of the world record for 100 metres
Sprinters within 10 seconds of the world record for 100 metres
Sprinters within 15 seconds of the world record for 100 metres

A respectable sprint school should aim to place *every* swimmer on the team on this board.

* Display thought-provoking sayings or mottoes in the changing rooms or the assembly area.
* Display a "thought for the week" on the top of the training blackboard.
* A simple "Meet Result" score board is worth considering. It has three headings with appropriate slots to record the information underneath: "Number of Wins", "Number of Consecutive Wins", "Number of Losses".
* A large general notice board is an essential and it is suggested that the coach's rules, the club rules and important telephone numbers be placed on it.
* If possible, set up your own "Swimming Hall of Fame" gallery with photographs of all your top performers, past and present.

Obviously, the above training equipment can only be permanently installed in long-term headquarters, but if you are not at that stage of development where you have a stable "home" pool, then you may present a lot of your motivating material as listed above by drawings, graphs, comparison charts and the like in a regular news bulletin, to all parents, swimmers and supporters.

Motivation makes medals. It is surprising how many corrugations in a swim club can be ironed out if everyone is motivated towards a single goal. The target becomes larger than the individual. Misunderstandings, petty jealousies, upset home schedules and minor inconveniences can all be smoothed over if the coach can stimulate and motivate the whole group.

5. A sprint plan for the junior team

Let the child's first lesson be obedience, and the second will be what thou wilt.

BENJAMIN FRANKLIN

This section is designed to cater for most of the needs of sprinters in the eight to thirteen years age range, that is the build-up years prior to national Age Group competitions. It can also be utilised by older sprinters who have limited time, or perhaps a country team, the Y.M.C.A. groups. The plan is constructed so the coach may add to it to meet advancing needs of pupils, for it contains all the essentials of an international schedule. You can apply this programme, with minor modifications to your team, knowing that you are on the right theme. The quality, the speed and the quantity have been reduced from that of an international workout. The basic ingredients are unaltered.

The pressure applied to each pupil by the coach is an individual assessment. This intangible cannot be put into print but commonsense is the keynote with the coach orchestrating the group according to their limits and their responses. Never lose sight of the fact that in the developing sprinter fun plays a part of training, controlled fun that is, and the length of the sprinter's swim life often depends on the hard but happy days in the developmental tank. Also, be mindful of the fact that in these formative years a general programme of all strokes, all distances, lays a better foundation than a specific freestyle only, sprint schedule. The latter may bring immediate results but who wants the world's fastest nine-year-old in preference to making the "big trip" one day. If this schedule has to have priorities they should be:

* Quality of technique in this first stage, and this I would rate as the prime essential for the developing sprinter, quality in the technique of all departments of all strokes; this is long term and may take two to three years to achieve.
* Secondly, I would place quality of the quantity; let all workouts, long or short, be infused with large doses of quality.

  Far better to schedule 4 × 400 metres efforts emphasising technique, good tumbles, negative splits, etc., than a 1,500 metres swim of dubious quality. Young sprinters cannot maintain quality all the way, well, the quality I am thinking of, two to three hours of quality concentration being just a little outside their capacities. The intelligent coach will have some low key sections where the emphasis is transferred from physical quality to mental quality. As an example: ten minutes trying to unravel the mysteries of a backstroke tumble turn is high quality concentration for most eight-year-olds with a low physical output. By moving the quality load from mental to physical and vice versa, the overall quality of the total workout is not impaired.

* Next I would stress continuity as a vital requirement. The student who can make ten or eleven sessions in a scheduled twelve each week must, by the laws of consistency and familiarity, have a better chance of success. Most sprinters in this age group do genuinely need a full-time physical outlet to satisfy their biological urges and surges. They need a physical balance to their mental school hours. Since continuity perfects a skill, and since the efficiency in skills reaches its peak after the age of twelve years, the more consistent we are in the formative years, the more efficient groove our neurological pathfinders will score out. Continuity counts most over the months and the years, not just the special bursts of one or two weeks.

This tripartite of technical perfection, quality in the workout and continuity cannot be bettered when constructing a sprint schedule.

Physiological Limitations: This junior work plan is purposely tailored to suit the growth needs of the junior. The physiological systems of younger children are apparently not so sufficiently developed to meet the demands of strenuous swimming as they become when puberty is reached. Children under the age of twelve years possess a highly active sympathetic nervous system which predisposes to a high heart rate and an easily depleted capacity for endurance activities such as swimming or running. Children under this age do not have the ability to utilise oxygen that older swimmers do, because of the relatively smaller stroke volume of the heart and a consequent capacity for increased circulation through the lungs. Young swimmers also possess a lesser supply of carbohydrate fuel, therefore the need for regular replenishment. Heart rates for the young are higher than the older conditioned pupil.

On the credit side, the ability of the swimmers to recover from strenuous work or repeated efforts reaches a peak very early, somewhere between the ages of twelve and fourteen years. This vitality declines significantly from the age of seventeen years, thus the need for older sprinters to have longer rest or recovery periods when the training pressure is at its peak and good times are expected. Coaches (and parents) are often astounded at the recovery ability of young swimmers (especially young girls) when repeating hard efforts, whilst older swimmers may be recording faster times but they appear "uncomfortable" in their performances.

The following schedules are very high in quantity and quality for a junior team. I have set a good standard as a step up for the top sprinter who wishes to do the senior workout.

Weeks 1, 2 and 3. (Adjusting to training for the new season).

* Compulsory for the pupils to attend a minimum of 8 out of the 10 sessions each week.
* Have 2 full rest days weekly.
* Do the weight training circuit 3 times weekly (see end of this chapter).

* Do 15 minutes of rubbers daily, 7 days a week (see end of this chapter).
* Commence log book, record height, weight, targets, general remarks, early morning heart rates.

MORNINGS, all strokes **Work**	**Distance**	**Total Time allowed**	**Effort %**
1,000 metres freestyle for technique	1,000		75
500 metres backstroke for technique	500		75
500 metres breaststroke for glide and turns	500		75
500 metres butterfly for as few stops as possible	500		75
1,000 metres tube pulling or legs tied, freestyle	1,000		85
10 × 100 metres freestyle kicking practice departing every 2 minutes, or 2 minutes 15 seconds	1,000		85
5 × 200 metres medleys departing every 3 minutes 30 seconds	1,000	5·5 km. 2 hours	
EVENINGS, slightly faster and more interesting work. **Work**			
4 × 10 × 50 metres freestyle sprints departing every 55 secs., each set being slightly faster than the previous set	2,000		80–90
10 × 100 metres medleys departing every 1 min 45 secs.	1,000		85
5 × 100 metres legs tied departing every 1 min 45 secs.	500		85
5 × 100 metres kick (any style) departing every 2 mins.	500		85
10 × 50 metres butterfly sprints departing every 60 secs.	500		90
		4·5 km. 1 hour 40 mins	

Grand totals for the first three weeks:

Exercise	Weight work	Swimming	Total	Distance
5·25 hours	4·5 hours	52 hours	61·75 hours	150 km.

Weeks 4, 5 and 6 (including new aids and lifting the work load).

* Attendance should now be 9 sessions out of 10 each week.
* Have 2 full rest days weekly.
* Do the weight training circuit 3 times weekly.
* Do 15 minutes on rubbers daily, 7 days a week.
* Check body weight and record, also early morning heart rates.

MORNINGS, basic conditioning.	Distance	Total	Time allowed	Effort %
Work				
5 × 400 metres freestyle departing every 6 mins.	2,000			85
10 × 100 metres freestyle kick sprints departing every 2 mins.	1,000			88
1,000 metres legs tied, non stop	1,000			85
10 × 200 medleys departing every 3 mins. 20 secs.	2,000			88
		6·0 km.	2 hours	

EVENINGS, picking up the speed a little.	Distance	Total	Time allowed	Effort %
Work				
1,000 metres fast freestyle with hand paddles	1,000			88
3 × 10 × 50 metres freestyle sprints going on the 50 secs. and making each set faster than the previous set	1,500			85–92
10 × 100 metres freestyle kick sprints with flippers departing every 1 min. 30 secs. and aiming to better 1 min. 15 secs.	1,000			95
2 × 10 × 50 metres butterfly sprints going every 60 secs.	1,000			90
10 × 50 metres legs tied sprints going every 60 secs. and aiming to better 40 secs.	500			95
		5·0 km.	1 hour 40 mins.	

Grand totals for 6 weeks:

Exercise	Weight work	Swimming	Total	Distance
10·5 hours	9 hours	104 hours	123·5 hours	315 km.

Weeks 7, 8 and 9 (applying pressure, a little specialisation).

* Sessions now go to 12 a week, with the pupil required to do 11.
* Rest days are Sundays and one morning each week, if the pupil genuinely requires it and as directed by the coach.
* Do weight training 3 times weekly but increase weights by 10 per cent.
* Do 15 minutes daily on rubbers, 7 days a week.
* Check body weight, early morning heart rate, record in log book. Quiz yourself as to schoolwork, projects, are you keeping pace or falling behind? Can you organise yourself a little better to cope with both loads, sport and school?

MORNINGS, the name of the game is 7,000 metres in 2 hours.	**Dis-tance**	**Total**	**Time allowed**	**Effort %**
Work				
10 × 200 metres freestyle sprints, departing every 2 mins. 45 secs. (you may use hand paddles in this section if you wish, perhaps every second morning)	2,000			90
10 × 100 metres freestyle kick sprints with flippers departing every 1 min. 30 secs. and aiming to better 1 min. 13 secs.	1,000			95
10 × 100 metres freestyle with legs tied departing every 1 min. 40 secs.	1,000			88
5 × 200 metres medleys departing every 3 mins 10 secs.	1,000			90
20 × 100 freestyle sprints or butterfly for the first 50 metres and freestyle for the second 50 metres throughout, departing every 1 min. 45 secs.	2,000			95
		7·0 km.	2 hours	
EVENINGS, a little light sprinting appears.				
Work				
Do this non stop, fast and in the right order: put on your hand paddles and your leg ties, then proceed with 500 metres freestyle. At the end of this 500 metres kick off your leg ties and proceed immediately with 500 metres of fast paddles. At the end of this second 500 metres slip off your paddles and proceed immediately with 500 metres fast freestyle. Time allowed for the 1,500 metres is 20 minutes	1,500			90
10 × 50 metres freestyle kick sprints departing every 60 secs. and aiming to better 45 secs.	500			95
10 × 50 metres butterfly sprints preferably, or any other secondary stroke, departing every 60 secs.	500			90
2 × 10 × 50 metres freestyle or butterfly sprints from dive start departing every 60 secs. (this means that coach will have to have the sprinters graduated correctly in each lane, fastest first through to slowest				

last). Aim to get to within 2·5 secs. of your best time for the 50 metres on as many as you can. Each dive to be a correctly executed start	1,000			97
20 × 25 metres freestyle sprints from dive departing every 30 secs. and trying to breathe only once or twice during each sprint. If pool is a 50 metres length then perhaps the sprints could be across the pool	500			97
20 × 50 metres sprints in the correct medley order departing every 50 or 55 secs.	1,000			93
		5·0 km.	1 hour 40 mins	

Grand totals for 9 weeks:

Exercise	Weight work	Swimming	Total	Distance
15·75 hours	13·5 hours	156 hours	185·25 hours	531·0 km.

Note that the mileage has increased at a steady rate every 3 weeks, that the effort percentage has increased also but the length of the sessions have remained the same. This allows the sprinter to adjust to the new season, schooling, home studies, some fun time, and the parents to transport, meals, etc. At the end of the ninth week just completed, the coach and pupils should have a complete break from the pool for three or four days. If the family can leave town for a long weekend of relaxation, all the better.

Week 10 (short week, long, fast work).

* Sessions are 6 only for this week, with the pupil to do them all.
* Weight sessions restricted to 2 only.
* Do 3 sessions of 15 minutes on rubbers for the week.
* Check body weight, height, early morning heart rate and record same in log book.
* Quiz yourself to see if you are happy in training, if there are any problems coach or parents can help you with. How is your schooling coming along?

MORNINGS, imagine that for this week you are a long distance champion.	**Dis-tance**	**Total**	**Time allowed**	**Effort %**
Work				
1,500 metres fast freestyle as an effort trying to better your time each morning for the 3 days	1,500			95
1,000 metres fast freestyle kick with flippers trying to better 16 mins.	1,000			95

1,500 metres freestyle with paddles, fast	1,500		90
5 × 400 metres medleys continuous (non stop) aiming to better 34 mins.	2,000		90
20 × 100 metres freestyle sprints departing every 1 min. 30 secs.	2,000		90
		8·0 km. 2 hours	

To be able to do this 8,000 metres in 2 hours is a fine achievement, if you fail, try again the next morning. Consider yourself a junior trainee worthy of any team if you succeed.

EVENINGS, still the long grind.

Work

3,000 metres fast non-stop freestyle, starting off at a steady and medium pace and progressively picking up speed until the last 800 metres is almost at full speed. Pupils working in "speed packs" can make for interesting training. Try to better your time each evening and although you are a sprinter, put up a respectable distance swim (under 40 mins.)	3,000		75–95
A fast 2,000 metres medley (that is, 500 metres of each of the 4 strokes non-stop)	2,000		90
		5·0 km. 1 hour 20 mins.	

Grand totals for 10 weeks:

Exercise	Weight work	Swimming	Total	Distance
16·50 hours	14·5 hours	166 hours	197 hours	570 km.

Weeks 11 and 12 (getting back into the sprint scene).

* Sessions are now stabilised at 12 a week, with the pupil required to do 11.
* Rest days are one full day and one morning sleep-in if the pupil genuinely requires it, and directed by the coach.
* Do weight training twice a week only from now on, but increase the weights by 10 per cent, that is, a total of 20 per cent since training commenced.
* Do 15 minutes on rubbers daily for 5 days, and do 2 sessions of 15 minutes each on Saturday and Sunday.
* Check and record body weight, height, early morning heart rates, your school performance. How is your swim style?

MORNINGS, you are halfway through the season so let us start quality work.	**Distance**	**Total**	**Time allowed**	**Effort %**
Work				
10 × 100 metres freestyle with hand paddles, departing every 1 min. 30 secs. and getting maximum "pull and shove" efficiency from the paddles	1,000			90
10 × 100 metres freestyle departing every 1 min. 30 secs., or if the junior team is very advanced, every 1 min. 20 secs. Each sprint to be 5 secs. away from your best time. The sprints have to be "negative splits", that is, the second 50 metres to be fractionally faster than the first 50 metres (e.g. 35 secs. plus 34 secs.)	1,000			95
250 metres of steady backstroke followed immediately by 250 metres of breaststroke, both for technique	500			75
10 × 100 metres freestyle kick sprints with the flippers, departing every 1 min. 30 secs. and aiming to better 1 min. 12 secs. Top junior sprinters can amaze with flipper-kick performances; I have seen juniors go as fast as 62 secs. out to 65 secs. in a repeat series	1,000			98
10 × 100 metres freestyle with legs tied or pulling a tube, departing every 1 min. 40 secs.	1,000			90
4 × 10 × 15 metres freestyle high power sprints (some sprints can be on another stroke in the early sets when the coach calls for a change, but the last two sets must be freestyle). Depart in descending time intervals, on the 55 secs., on the 50 secs., on the 45 secs., and the last set on the 40 secs.	2,000			88–95
		6·5 km.	2 hours	

EVENINGS, come on you sprint specialists, let's go.				
Work				
5 × 200 metres medleys departing every 3 mins. 15 secs. and getting progressively faster until the last effort is within 7 secs. of your personal best	1,000			85–95

20 × 50 metres kick sprints departing every 60 secs. and trying to better 45 secs. all the time	1,000	95
5 × 200 metres freestyle with the legs tied, departing every 3 mins. 15 secs., the times to become progressively faster	1,000	85–95
2 × 10 × 50 metres freestyle or butterfly sprints departing every 80 secs. from dive, These to be superior quality with correct dives. Aim to get to within 2 secs. of your personal best time for every sprint.	1,000	98
250 metres of steady backstroke followed immediately by 250 metres of breaststroke, both for technique	500	75
4 × 10 × 25 metres of butterfly sprints from push or drive departing every 30 secs. from push or every 40 secs. from dive. Keep quality high; do these sprints across the pool if more convenient	1,000	90–95
	5·5 km.	1 hour 50 mins.

Grand totals for 12 weeks:

Exercise	Weight work	Swimming	Total	Distance
18·75 hours	16·5 hours	212 hours	247·25 hours	714 km.

Weeks 13, 14 and 15 (the meat in the sandwich weeks).

* Sessions are now 12 for the week in general practice plus one special session of starts, turns, finishes and stroking when called for by the coach. Although stroke correction has been going on in the general sessions all these weeks, a little special attention is necessary for individual problems from time to time.
* Rest days are one full day weekly plus another morning off if required and directed by the coach.
* Weight sessions are twice weekly.
* Do 15 minutes on the rubbers daily for 5 days, with "double" periods of a weekend.
* Check and record weight, height, early morning heart rate. Check back on last year's log book at this stage and compare weight, height, competition times, school marks. Are you progressing satisfactorily? Is your general health all right? Do you still enjoy training even though it is getting harder?

MORNINGS, work now calls for a little more concentration.	Distance	Total	Time allowed	Effort %
Work				
5 × 400 metres freestyle efforts with hand paddles departing every 6 mins. and getting to within 15 secs. for your best 400 metres time on all efforts	2,000			90–95
500 metres freestyle kicking in less than 9 mins.	500			93
5 × 200 metres freestyle efforts departing every 3 mins and aiming to swim within 8 secs. of your best time	1,000			95
500 metres freestyle with legs tied in less than 7 mins. 30 secs.	500			90
10 × 100 metres freestyle departing every 1 min. 25 secs.	1,000			90
30 × 50 metres sprints departing every 50 or 55 secs. and doing the sprints in the correct medley order	1,500			90
		6·5 km.	1 hour 45 mins.	
EVENINGS, shorter and faster work.				
Work				
4 × 10 × 50 metres freestyle sprints each set departing on the 50 secs., 50 secs., 45 secs. and 40 secs.	2,000			90–95
5 × 200 metres medleys departing every 3 mins. 15 secs.	1,000			90
2 × 10 × 50 metres freestyle sprints with the legs tied, each set departing on the 55 secs. and 50 secs.	1,000			90–95
2 × 10 × 50 metres freestyle kick sprints each set departing on the 60 secs. and 55 secs.	1,000			90–95
2 × 20 × 25 metres butterfly or freestyle sprints (or sprints across the pool) departing every 25 secs. from push	1,000			90–95
3 man relay of 10 × 50 metres freestyle at maximum speed: the whole team to participate, if pool space is not available try 3 man relay × 20 × across the pool	500			99
		6·5 km.	2 hours	

Grand totals for 15 weeks:

Exercises	Weight work	Swimming	Total	Distance
25·50 hours	19·50 hours	312·75 hours	357·75 hours	948 km.

Weeks 16, 17 and 18 (the last weeks before the polish-up).

* Sessions remain at 12 a week for the full squad with the possibility of an extra session for starts, turns, relay takeovers, finishes, technique if needed.
* Rest days are one a week, with a "sleep in" morning if the coach feels that it is warranted.
* Weight sessions remain at 2 a week.
* Do 15 minutes of "rubbers" daily for 5 week days, with double sessions on the weekends.
* At the commencement of the sixteenth week, if the coach so advises, have a haemoglobin level taken by your sports medicine doctor. Have this count interpreted to estimate if the stress upon you needs adjusting. Record weight and height, early morning heart rates.

MORNINGS, less work—higher quality.	**Distance**	**Total**	**Time allowed**	**Effort %**
Work				
10 × 100 metres freestyle sprints in descending steps of speed, 1–3, 4–6, 7–10 departing every 2 mins.	1,000			90–96
10 × 100 metres freestyle kick sprints aiming to better 1 min. 35 secs., departing every 3 mins.	1,000			96
10 × 100 metres freestyle sprints as "negative splits", i.e. the second 50 metres to be faster than the first 50 metres, with hand paddles departing every 2 mins.	1,000			95
10 × 100 metres freestyle sprints with the legs tied departing every 2 mins. and to be done in descending sets of speed, 1–3, 4–6, 7–10	1,000			90–96
30 × 50 metres sprints going up the pool on butterfly, going down the pool on freestyle, departing every 60 secs. and working within 3·5 secs. of your personal best times	1,500			95
		5·5 km.	2 hours	

EVENINGS, less work, super sprints, some fun.				
Work				
2 × 10 × 50 metres freestyle sprints from dive departing every 80 secs.	1,000			96
20 "doubles", i.e. sprints across the				

pool and back with a correct racing start and a fast tumble turn, sprints to be absolute maximum until the "pain in the side" comes on, departing every 60 secs. (for 40 yards or 40 metres)	800	100
1 × 200 metres medley in 2 mins. 45 secs.	200	85
2 × 10 × 50 metres kick sprints with the flippers, working the first set of 10 on freestyle kick and the second set on dolphin kick. Depart every 60 secs. and work at full speed up the pool and 95 per cent down the pool	1,000	95–100
2 × 10 × 50 metres freestyle sprints with the legs tied departing every 60 secs.	1,000	95
20 × 25 metres freestyle sprints swum in the polo style, i.e. with the face looking over the water in front and not turning the head from side to side to breathe. Depart every 30 secs. (or do these as across the pool sprints)	500	95
1 × 50 metres freestyle sprint from dive, timed by coach in an attempt on your best time. Each evening alter this sprint to another stroke, or a kick sprint, legs tied sprint, etc	50	100
	4·5 km.	1 hour 45 mins.

Grand totals for 18 weeks:

Exercises	Weight work	Swimming	Total	Distance
32·25 hours	22·50 hours	380·25 hours	435 hours	1,128 km.

Weeks 19 and 20 (you are now reaching your "peak" in condition for this half-year season but not your "peak" in speed).

* Sessions come down to 11 a week, but all pupils must attend all sessions. Coach may call for a special 1 hour session on stroke or details as an extra.
* Rest days, 1 full rest day weekly and 1 sleep-in morning, possibly after race night.
* Weight sessions remain at 2 a week.
* Continue the daily 15 minutes on "rubbers" with a double session at the weekends.
* As we are about to enter the final stage of the season make sure that

you have everything under control, i.e. your school projects and school work are up to date, you are in good health, sleeping well, eating well, you are happy and not too worried, you have no sore ears, worrysome teeth, not so tired that you go to sleep in school, etc. In other words, you are going to make sure that you will be the fittest and healthiest sprinter entering this last 6 weeks period. Record weight and height and have coach analyse them. Take early morning heart rates. Ask coach if there are any supplementary foods or "extras" you should be having.

MORNINGS, lifting to new levels.	**Distance**	**Total**	**Time allowed**	**Effort %**
Work				
12 × 50 metres freestyle sprints departing every 60 secs. and increasing the speed as you warm up	600			85–95
1 × 400 metres effort at maximum speed, each morning to do a different effort, i.e. medley, backstroke, kicking, kicking with flippers, pulling, etc. Record these times for next season's reference as they represent your "peak condition performances"	400			100
10 × 50 metres freestyle kick sprints departing every 1 min. 30 secs. and aiming for sub-40 secs.	500			96
10 × 50 metres freestyle sprints with the legs tied departing every 1 min. 15 secs. and aiming to better 35 secs.	500			96
250 metres backstroke at a steady speed followed immediately by 250 metres breaststroke for style	500			85
10 × 100 metres freestyle sprints from dive departing every 2 mins. and trying for "negative splits". All sprints to be within 6 secs. of your personal best	1,000			95
3 × 10 × 50 metres freestyle sprints departing every 40 secs; starting off steady and finishing hard onto the wall	1,500			95
		5·0 km.	1 hour 40 mins.	

EVENINGS, 5,000 metres at greater than 93 per cent effort.

Work

16 × 50 metres freestyle sprints departing every 60 secs. and increasing

the effort as you warm up 1 × 200 metres effort at maximum speed. Each evening do a different effort, i.e. medley, butterfly, pull, kick, freestyle, etc. Record these times for future reference	200	100
2 × 10 × 50 metres freestyle sprints with hand paddles departing every 1 min. 15 secs. and aiming to get to within 3 secs. of your personal best time on all sprints	1,000	96
2 × 10 × 25 butterfly sprints departing every 30 secs. and breathing every three strokes, going near to maximum effort (or the equivalent across the pool sprints)	500	98
2 × 10 × 50 metres freestyle kick sprints (with or without flippers at coach's discretion) departing every 1 min. 30 secs. and working near maximum speed	1,000	96
2 × 10 × 25 metres sprints in the medley order departing every 30 secs. at near maximum speed (or the equivalent in across the pool sprints)	500	95
3 man relay × 20 × 50 metres freestyle, i.e. each sprinter to do 20 sprints of 50 metres. Each team to try to better 31 minutes with the very best teams under 30 minutes; all from dive with correct takeovers and penalties placed on teams "breaking"	1,000	98
	5·0 km.	2 hours 20 mins.

Grand totals for 20 weeks:

Exercises	Weight work	Swimming	Total	Distance
36·75 hours	24·50 hours	424·91 hours	486·16 hours	1,242 km

Note. If pool allotment time does not allow for 2 hours 20 minutes in the evening, either cut down the 3 man relay or change the morning programme to the evening and vice versa.

Weeks 21 and 22 (if you have done all your work diligently to this point, you have no worries from here on).

* Sessions come down to 10 a week and you are expected to be at them all.
* Weight training is down to one a week and it should be done on a rest morning.
* "Rubber" workouts revert to one 15 minute session for the seven days of each week.
* Wherever possible try to take a middle of the day sleep.
* As you enter the first stage of taper down it is important to watch health, body weight (no increases now) and take "cat naps" whenever convenient. Early morning heart rates should now be near their all time low, you should be right on your best racing weight. Now is the time to start getting extra close to coach and starting to work on your final race plans and imitating them in training.

MORNINGS, entering the "count down" stage.	**Distance**	**Total**	**Time allowed**	**Effort %**
Work				
3 × 10 × 50 metres freestyle sprints each set departing on the 60 secs., 50 secs., 40 secs.	1,500			95
10 × 50 metres kick sprints departing every 1 min. 30 secs. and aiming to better 39 secs.	500			97
10 "broken" 100 metres freestyle sprints departing every 2 mins. and going up the pool hard for style and coming back down faster. (Broken sprints means have a 5 or 10 secs. rest interval at the 50 metres mark according to coach's instructions)	1,000			95
10 × 50 metres freestyle sprints with the legs tied departing every 1 min. 30 secs. and aiming to better 34 secs.	500			97
10 "special" 100 metres freestyle sprints departing every 3 mins. in descending steps of speed, 1–3, 4–6, 7–10. For a ((1·00" sprinter I would expect a 67, 67, 67, then a 64, 64, 64, with the final 4 sprints at maximum speed trying to get near the 60 secs.	1,000			90–100
Starts, turns, finishes				
		4·5 km.	1 hour 40 mins.	

EVENINGS, injecting the "sparkle". **Work**	**Distance**	**Total**	**Time allowed**	**Effort %**
2 × 10 × 25 metres freestyle or butterfly sprints departing every 25 secs. (or across the pool sprints)	500			95
3 × 5 × 100 metres freestyle sprints in descending steps of speed, 1–3, 4–6, 7–10, departing every 2 mins.	1,500			90–97
5 × 100 metres freestyle kick sprints departing every 3 mins. and aiming to better 1 min. 35 secs.	500			97
5 × 100 metres freestyle sprints with the legs tied departing every 2 mins. and aiming to better 1 min. 20 secs.	500			95
2 × 10 × 25 metres freestyle sprints from dive trying to better 12·5 secs. for boys and 13·3 secs. for girls, on as many sprints as possible	500			98
3 man × 10 times 50 metres freestyle relay (i.e. each sprinter to do 10 sprints of 50 metres) Each team to try to better 15 mins. All teams to be under 16 mins. with penalties for teams "breaking"	500			100
Short speed bursts, turns, starts, take-overs, etc.	500			90–100
		4·5 km.	1 hour 50 mins.	

Grand totals for 22 weeks:

Exercises	Weight work	Swimming	Total	Distance
38·50 hours	25·50 hours	459·91 hours	523·91 hours	

Week 23 (into the home stretch)

* Only 9 sessions this week. One full rest day, and Tuesday, Thursday and Saturday mornings sleep in. Students must attend all sessions.
* Only one weight workout for the week, on Thursday morning.
* Do one 15 minute session on "rubbers" daily for the 7 days.
* Sleep in the middle of the day, as well as 8–9 hours every night.
* As the schedule allows for more free time (and a build-up of energy reserves) do not be tempted into expending your energies on unusual activities, lead a very normal life. Check early morning heart rate, body weight, height. Ask coach if you are swimming to expectations.

A sprint plan for the junior team

MORNINGS, make every stroke, every turn, every start, the best you know how.

Work	**Distance**	**Total**	**Time allowed**	**Effort %**
2 × 10 × 25 metres freestyle sprints departing every 30 secs. (or across the pool sprints)	500			95
2 × 10 × 50 metres freestyle sprints departing every 60 secs. First set for perfect style, the second set for near maximum effort	1,000			90–99
2 × 10 × 100 metres freestyle sprints departing every 2 mins., the first set to be 10 secs. away from your personal best time, the second set to be 5 secs. slower than your best	2,000			90–95
2 × 10 × 25 metres freestyle sprints from dive trying to better 12·3 secs. for the boys and 13·1 secs. for the girls, on as many sprints as possible	500			100
A series of flat out tumble turns		4·0 km.	1 hour 30 mins.	

EVENINGS, 10, 9, 8, 7, 6, 5 –

Work				
1 × 10 × 25 metres butterfly departing every 30 secs.	250			95
1 × 10 × 25 metres freestyle sprints breathing only once or twice in each sprint, departing every 30 secs.	250			95
2 × 200 metres freestyle sprints, one every 5 mins. and aiming to equal your best time for the distance. Swim them with negative splits	400			100
6 "broken" 100 metres freestyle sprints departing every 3 mins. and aiming for a faster second lap than the first lap. ("broken" to mean 10 secs. rest at the 50 metres mark)	600			96
3 man relay across the pool (20 yards or 20 metres) each man to swim 20 times at maximum speed, with correct dive starts and takeovers and finishes	400			100
12 × 50 metres freestyle sprints from dive departing every 2 mins. and aiming to get within 1·2 secs. of your				

personal best time on as many as possible	600			99
2 × 10 × 25 metres freestyle sprints from dive, departing every 2 mins. and aiming to get within 1·2 secs. of your personal best time on as many as possible	600			99
2 × 10 × 25 metres freestyle sprints from dive start trying to better 12·1 secs. for the boys and 13·0 secs. for the girls on as many sprints as possible	500			100
Starts, turns, takeovers as directed		3·5 km.	1 hour 30 mins.	

Grand totals for 23 weeks:

Exercises	Weight work	Swimming	Total	Distance
40·25 hours	26·0 hours	473·41 hours	539·66 hours	1,362 km.

Week 24, final taper.

* Sessions adjusted to your competition requirements for this vital week, but normally 7 or 8 sessions. In this instance assume that you are swimming heats on Saturday morning and finals on Saturday night.
* Weight training to be done once only for the week on the Monday or Tuesday.
* Do your "rubber" exercises for 10 minutes only every day this week.
* Sleep in the middle of the day, as well as 9 hours each night.
* Do your final weight check (every day) and your early morning heart rate count and record same. Finalise your race plan and approach with coach this week. Do not wait until the last few hours when he may be busy with the senior swimmers, unless directed to do so.

MONDAY MORNING, 4, 3, 2, 1, blast off.	**Distance**	**Total**	**Time allowed**	**Effort %**
Work				
2 × 10 × 50 metres freestyle departing on the 60 secs. for the first set and on the 45 secs. for the second set. Style and speed	1,000			85–95
10 × 100 metres freestyle sprints departing every 1 min. 30 secs. and descending in steps of speed, 1–3, 4–6, 7–10	1,000			85–90–95
500 metres steady to fast freestyle kick	500			85

500 metres steady to fast freestyle with legs tied	500	85
2 × 10 × 25 metres freestyle sprints from push, departing every 30 secs. and working near race pace	500	95
5 × 100 metres freestyle sprints as a special effort departing every 3 mins. from dive and attempting to do your best series ever	500	97–100
Practise starts, turns, technique, etc	4·0km	1 hour 30 mins

MONDAY EVENING

Work

2 × 10 × 25 metres freestyle sprints from dive start	500	98
3 man relay × 10 × 50 metres freestyle (i.e. each sprinter to swim 10 × 50 metres). The teams will attempt to set pool records for the various ages and sexes	500	100
20 racing turns from 10 metres out from the side wall, for the complete team as a competition in which the last person to return to the 10 metres mark is eliminated, until the last boy and the last girl remain for the "finals"	400	100
2 × 200 metres freestyle sprints departing every 5 mins. from push and both swims to be within 5 secs. of your personal best time	400	96
1 × 200 metres medley as a relaxer	200	80
3 man relay across the pool (20 × 20 yds. or 20 × 20 metres) i.e. each man to swim 20 sprints across the pool. The relay to be on the medley strokes	400	97
3 man relay across the pool (20 × 20 yds. or 20 × 20 metres) i.e. each man to swim 20 sprints across the pool on freestyle at maximum speed. Dive start	400	100
	2·8 km.	1 hour 30 mins.

TUESDAY MORNING, sleep in, no training.

TUESDAY EVENING, a repeat of the Monday evening programme in which all times you did on Monday have to be bettered.

WEDNESDAY MORNING **Work**	**Distance**	**Total**	**Time allowed**	**Effort %**
500 metres freestyle kicking at a good speed	500			85
500 metres freestyle with the legs tied at a good speed	500			85
10 × 100 metres freestyle sprints as "negative splits" departing every 3 mins. and all swims to be within 5 secs. of your personal best time	1,000			95
200 metres medley as a relaxer	200			80
10 × 50 metres freestyle sprints from dive departing every 1 min. 30 secs. All sprints to be within 1·5 secs. of your personal best time	500			97
2 × 10 × 25 metres special sprints of freestyle from dive in which the boys will have to try to better 12 secs. for as many sprints as possible, and the girls aim to better 13 secs.	500			100
A dozen or so sprints across under the eye of the coach for starting technique	300			95
		3·5 km.	1 hour 30 mins.	

WEDNESDAY EVENING **Work**	**Distance**	**Total**	**Time allowed**	**Effort %**
500 metres freestyle for style at a steady pace with the coach watching out for any stroke faults	500			85
500 metres freestyle kick at a steady speed	500			85
5 × 100 metres freestyle sprints as "negative splits" departing every 3 mins. Efforts to be 85%, 90%, 97%, 95%, 90%	500			85–97
3 man relay across the pool in which each man swims 20 times (3 man × 20 × 20 metres). Freestyle and from dive start. Pool record attempts	400			100
6 × 50 metres freestyle sprints from dive departing every 3 mins., the first 25 metres going hard for style perfection and the last 25 metres, flat out	300			98
Turns, finishes, takeovers		2·2 km.	1 hour 15 mins.	

THURSDAY, complete rest day, often the day for travel to meets. Some swimmers like to sleep in on this day and take a light relaxing swim in the evening; it helps them to sleep at night.

FRIDAY MORNING

Work			
500 metres freestyle at a steady pace with coach watching technique	500		85
5 × 100 metres freestyle sprints departing every 3 mins. with the sprinter trying to swim to within 8 secs. of his personal best time	500		88
500 metres steady freestyle kick	500		85
2 × 10 × 25 metres freestyle sprints not quite flat out, but with emphasis on the way the first 25 metres of tomorrow's race will be swum	500		95
		2·0 km. 1 hour	

FRIDAY EVENING

Work			
A rest evening for those who prefer not to swim on the eve of a long day (possibly the ectomorphs), but for others who prefer the tension of a long day to be broken and to aid in the evening's sleep, a light session and a final "talk down" by coach. 500 metres freestyle for style at a steady pace	500		85
10 × 25 metres freestyle at a rollicking speed but not flat out. From dive	250		95
turns, and sprints in from 15 metres for a finish	250		90
10 × 20 metres sprints across the pool, freestyle with a correct racing start (gun or hooter) and with a tumble turn at the end of the sprint	200		95
300 metres relaxing swim with your team mates just for fun	300		80
		1·5 km. 1 hour	

Grand totals for the season of 24 weeks:

Exercises	Weight work	Swimming	Total	Distance
41·41 hours	26·50 hours	482·66 hours	550·57 hours	1,381 km.

Weekly averages for the 6 months season are:

Exercises	Weight work	Swimming	Total	Distance
1·66 hours	1·1 hours	20 hours	23 hours	57·5 km

and all serious junior trainees must attain this standard at least, to succeed.

A suggested exercise programme for the Junior Sprinter.
15 minutes on stretch rubbers.

Freestyle Arm Action. Do the complete arm cycle, emphasise a high elbow action, take care to co-ordinate the timing cycle correctly, keep the wrists firm. Do 10 sets of 30 seconds and on each set work progressively faster and with a greater stretch on the rubbers.

Butterfly Arm Action. Do the full arm cycle, pull, push and recovery. Keep well bent over from the waist, keep the head down and concentrate on correct technique. Do 10 sets of 30 seconds and on each set work faster. In the 3 major positions of the pull i.e.

(a) the first press,
(b) the midway pull,
(c) the press back, do 5 isometrics each of 5 seconds as an isometric for the 3 positions.

Backstroke Arm Action. Lying on a bench in a supine position, do 10 sets of 30 seconds of the complete backstroke arm action, with emphasis on the push section of the stroke. Co-ordinate perfectly by commencing slowly and building up speed.

Freestyle Arm Action as an Isometric. In the 3 main positions of the stroke,

(a) first press,
(b) mid line under umbilicus press,
(c) end of stroke push, do 5 isometrics each of 5 seconds for the 3 positions on each arm.

Weight training with barbell (use a weight in pounds, approximately 3 times your age in years as a rough guide).

Lift and Press. Lift the barbell from a comfortable standing position. Keep wrists curled out. Lift the weight above the head and straighten legs at the same time. Return weight to floor.
Repetitions: 3 sets of 10 movements.

Horizontal Pullovers. Lying on the floor in a supine position with the arms extended behind the head, slowly lift the bar up to the vertical. Keep knees bent. Keep arms shoulder width apart. Return the bar to the floor. You may need assistance to lift the weight in the early stages of this programme.
Repetitions: 3 sets of 10 movements.

Half Squats. Standing with the feet apart and the barbell comfortably on the shoulders, bend the knees forward until you assume a half squatting position. Keep heels on floor. Return to the upright position. This exercise is not hard and heavier weights may be used.

Repetitions: 2 sets of 10 movements.
French Curl. From a standing or kneeling position and with the barbell held overhead and the hands fairly close together, slowly bend the elbows until the bar is on your neck. Keep the upper trunk straight. Then straighten the elbows until the bar returns to the original position. Keep the elbows tucked in tightly to the side of the head throughout the exercise. This exercise is hard and you may need assistance to move the weight early in the programme or a lighter weight may be used.
Repetitions: 3 sets of 10 movements.
Back Lifts. In a standing position with the trunk slightly bent forward and the barbell held behind the buttocks, press the weight backwards and upwards as far as possible. Return to starting position.
Arm Rotators. Lying on the back with the arms bent at right angles so that the barbell is on the floor, almost touching the back of your head, slowly raise the bar to the vertical and return it to the floor. Keep the elbows on the floor throughout. The forearms and hands are the only parts of the body to leave the floor.
Repetitions: 3 sets of 10 movements.
Wrist Curls. Sitting on a chair and bending forward with forearms resting on the thighs, flex and extend the wrists and fingers, making the barbell roll backwards and forwards. Either a barbell or two dumb-bells may be used.
Repetitions: 3 sets of 10 movements on each hand

6. The London Papers

Chapters on training schedules I have seen in swimming literature tend to set out the "ideal". Coaches and swimmers know that rarely, if ever, can the team comply with the work as set down on paper. Illnesses, pool closures, study or examinations, weather conditions, transport breakdowns and taper, are only a few of the many reasons why pupils do not duplicate written weekly schedules. Coaches pre-determine the desired load of the daily or weekly work sheet. If you can achieve a 90 per cent result in attendance and work accomplished, you are doing the very best possible. Actually, I am not satisfied, but have to be content with, just above 85 per cent of attendance and work completed by the top team.

This does not necessarily mean the swimmers do only eight workouts out of the ten each week. It means that over an extended period, a week lost for any of the above reasons lowers the percentages dramatically. At present, my team is working between 70,000 and 80,000 yards a week and although this "small amount" will be frowned upon by some Australian and New Zealand coaches, it is in line with the North American scene. It is as good as they can do in the twenty hours allotted pool time and still maintain quality. If more than a dozen swimmers reach the target each week I consider it a good performance. In the lower age groups the percentages are higher because the hours and mileages are less.

This chapter shows what actually does happen within most teams, and although top coaches may read this and nod agreement younger coaches will be heartened to know that 90 per cent of your workload completed, or pupils in attendance, is as good as you could wish for. Better figures usually result during school holidays.

NOTE: In September, 1975, I was engaged by the London "Y" Aquatic Club, Ontario, Canada, for the specific purpose of raising the standard in this once famous swim club. I had to coach the coaches and if I could produce swimmers for the national level, so much the better. The two hundred members were relegated into graded teams and I took control of the top group. The team had rarely worked beyond 8,000 yards daily, their mileage for the previous twelve months being 560. My first task was to update the techniques, improve the conditioning, introduce land training, set personal targets and create a feeling of purpose. From the top team I selected a group of six swimmers with apparent potential to form a special squad, but I left my options open in case I had chosen incorrectly. The four boys had an average time of 55·8 seconds for the 100 yards, the girls, 57·6 seconds. This team worked in lanes separate from the rest of the squad, but at the same time. Each swimmer was given a work sheet weekly. (The "Confidential" heading was placed on the work sheet to give the pupils a feeling of being special).

Work Sheet No. 1. Confidential

September 15, 1975

Dear Swimmers,

You have been selected to form a special squad. I know that you are all capable of reaching national class and perhaps beyond. You are warned that you must become very serious about this experiment. You must now generate a whole new outlook towards training and competition. Your present workload will be doubled, the quality upgraded. If you feel during the following weeks the pressure is too great, or that your schooling or health is starting to suffer, report to me and we will try to work out a solution. However, if you are not working to the required standard because you are not capable, I will place you back into the general squad. This is not a disgrace. The way you accept this reverse, if indeed you are put down, will show me the qualities of your character. You must, by hard work, aim to get back into the special squad as soon as possible.

The general team has been set 5,000 yards for the morning workouts. We will commence our first week at 6,000 yards for the six mornings. This is not as much work as Point Claire, Vancouver or Thunder Bay are doing, but for your start-off week it will be a reasonable load, especially as we will be working on technique. I want you to get into the water as soon as you arrive on the deck. Your programme will be written up, the equipment set out, there will be no need to leave the water until the session ends.

The afternoon workouts will be 5,000 metres on the Monday, Wednesday and Friday. We will try for 4,000 metres in the one hour allocated pool time on the Tuesday and Thursday. Saturday afternoon will be for land work. Sunday will be a rest day except for competitions. I expect you to handle the 61,300 yards for the week. Quality more than yardage will be our theme.

Morning Programme, Monday, Wednesday and Friday

1. 500 yards of Swim, Kick, Pull on freestyle as a warm up (In S.K.P. you swim one lap, kick one lap, pull one lap, alternately.)
2. 30 × 100 yards of your main stroke on the 1 min. 30 secs. (Short rest at 15). Freestylers aim for 63—65 seconds.
3. 1,000 yards legs tied with bands either on freestyle or backstroke. This must be done fast and without stopping.
4. 30 × 50 yards sprints with hand paddles on freestyle departing every 45 seconds and aiming to swim between 29 and 31 seconds.

Morning total—6,000 yards

Afternoon Programme, Monday, Wednesday and Friday

1. 500 metres of Swim, Kick, Pull on breaststroke as a warm up.
2. 10 × 400 metres efforts, departing every 6 minutes. Freestylers to

better 4 mins. 50 secs. all the time, backstrokers and I.M. swimmers to better 5 mins. 45 secs.
Afternoon total—5,000 metres

Morning Programme, Tuesday, Thursday and Saturday

1. 500 yards Swim, Kick, Pull on backstroke as a warm up.
2. 15 × 200 yards freestyle departing every 2 mins. 45 secs. and working at a very hard rate. Freestylers aim for 2 mins. 6 secs. or less.
3. 500 yards breaststroke at a lively speed.
4. 20 × 100 yards of individual medley departing every 1 min. 30 secs. Try to better 1 min. 12 secs.

Morning total—6,000 yards

Afternoon Programme, Tuesday and Thursday

1. 3,000 metres freestyle starting off at a steady rate and picking up speed, aiming to go under 5 minutes for each 400 metres.
2. 40 × 25 metres butterfly departing every 25 seconds and breathing every 3 strokes as much as possible.

Afternoon total—4,000 metres
Weekly total—61,000 yards

Work Sheet No. 2. Confidential

September 22, 1975.

Dear Swimmers,
Our first week was one of mixed fortunes. You certainly tried hard and I am satisfied with the effort. Unfortunately, only two achieved the target of 61,300 yards, due to time out for study and approaching school exams. Nevertheless, everyone swam further than 50,000 yards and I found out that Vancouver usually starts the winter season gradually, so at this point we are ahead of this fine team. Alan, I am concerned about your sore shoulder. Do not swim butterfly or legs tied this coming week. We will substitute kicking instead and see if your deltoids improve.

You are all friends and yet rivals in the water, therefore, you should know that it will be the better use of your intelligence and determination that will decree who is to have the fittest swim body. It will be the constant pressure applied to your efforts and the constant thought applied to your stroke that wins out in the long run. Work harder, think smarter than your lane mate and the odds move in your favour. For example, if the programme calls for 10 × 400s you should aim to work to within 10 seconds of your best time for the distance on each swim, with an occasional one eased back a little to concentrate on technique.

I have introduced kicking with flippers this week. Since kicking is so essential and our pool time so limited we will work with flippers.

You will find that this is a most beneficial exercise with one proviso—it must be done at maximum speed. You will need to wear socks under your flippers because of the occurance of blisters and rubbing. Training is maintained at 61,300 yards for the week but this time everyone will reach the target.

This week I have attached a chart which will give you an indication of your relative position in the nation. This chart has been produced by the Canadian Swimming Association. The "national standard" column represents the qualifying times for the summer nationals. All members of our special squad fall within the +15% to +7% columns. Although you are age-group swimmers we must aim for the times listed in this senior swimmers' chart. National selectors take notice of recorded times when selecting teams, the age of swimmer does not figure too largely in their calculations. Vancouver, Quebec, Thunder Bay and Toronto teams are all in the minus per cent columns. It will be our plan to reach national standard as quickly as possible and then go out after the leading groups.

Morning Programme, Monday, Wednesday and Friday

1. 500 yards of S.K.P. on breaststroke as your warm up.
2. 2 × 1,500 yards efforts at +90% with 30 seconds rest between each. The second 1,500 to be faster than the first.
3. 1,500 yards freestyle or backstroke with the legs tied. If shoulders are strong and have no signs of soreness, do it very hard.
4. 20 × 50 yards sprints in the medley order throughout and departing every 45 seconds.

Morning total—6,000 yards

Afternoon Programme, Monday, Wednesday and Friday

1. 500 metres S.K.P. on freestyle.
2. 10 × 300 metres freestyle sprints departing every 4 minutes and trying to do as many sprints as possible under 3 mins. 30 secs.
3. 500 metres breaststroke at a good pace.
4. 5 × 200 metres legs tied departing every 3 minutes.

Afternoon total—5,000 metres

Morning Programme, Tuesday, Thursday and Saturday

1. 500 yards S.K.P. on backstroke.
2. 20 × 100 yards freestyle trying to hold a steady pace all the way. Depart every 1 min. 20 secs. Paula, try for 62s, Alan and Bill aim for 61s.
3. 500 yards steady butterfly non stop.
4. 20 × 100 yards freestyle legs tied, departing every 1 min. 30 secs.
5. 10 × 100 yards flipper kick sprints with boards departing every 1 min. 30 secs. and aiming for 66 seconds.

Morning total—6,000 yards

COMPARATIVE PERCENTAGE CHART MEN (Canada 1976)

LONG COURSE METRES

	−5%	−3%	−2%	−1%	**National Standard**	+1%	+2%	+3%	+4%	+5%	+7%	+10%	+15%
100 free	54·0	55·2	55·7	56·3	**56·85**	57·5	58·0	58·6	59·2	59·7	1:00·8	1:02·6	1:05·4
200 free	1:58·0	1:59·2	2:00·4	2:01·6	**2:02·78**	2:04·0	2:05·2	2:06·4	2:07·6	2:08·8	2:11·2	2:14·8	2:20·8
400 free	4:06·3	4:11·5	4:14·1	4:16·7	**4:19·30**	4:21·9	4:24·5	4:27·1	4:29·7	4:32·3	4:37·5	4:45·3	4:58·3
800 free	8:36·5	8:47·3	8:52·7	8:58·1	**9:03·48**	9:08·9	9:14·3	9:19·7	9:25·1	9:30·5	9:41·3	9:57·5	10:24·5
1500 free	16:14·9	16:35·5	16:45·8	16:56·1	**17:06·44**	17:16·7	17:27·0	17:37·3	17:47·6	17:57·9	18:18·5	18:49·4	19:40·9
100 back	1:01·6	1:02·8	1:03·4	1:04·0	**1:04·66**	1:05·2	1:05·8	1:06·4	1:07·0	1:07·6	1:08·8	1:10·6	1:13·6
200 back	2:14·2	2:17·0	2:18·4	2:19·8	**2:21·20**	2:22·6	2:24·0	2:25·4	2:26·8	2:29·2	2:32·0	2:36·2	2:43·2
100 breast	1:09·3	1:10·7	1:11·4	1:12·1	**1:12·88**	1:13·6	1:14·3	1:15·0	1:15·7	1:16·4	1:17·8	1:19·9	1:23·4
200 breast	2:30·8	2:34·0	2:35·6	2:37·2	**2:38·82**	2:40·4	2:42·0	2:43·6	2:45·2	2:46·8	2:50·0	2:54·8	3:02·8
100 fly	58·9	1:00·1	1:00·7	1:01·3	**1:01·9**	1:02·5	1:03·1	1:03·7	1:04·3	1:04·9	1:06·1	1:07·9	1:10·9
200 fly	2:09·5	2:12·3	2:13·7	2:15·1	**2:16·52**	2:17·9	2:19·3	2:20·7	2:22·1	2:23·5	2:26·3	2:30·5	2:37·5
200 im	2:12·5	2:15·3	2:16·7	2:18·1	**2:19·52**	2:20·9	2:22·3	2:23·7	2:25·1	2:26·5	2:29·3	2:33·5	2:40·5
400 im	4:46·2	4:49·2	4:52·2	4:55·2	**4:58·19**	5:01·2	5:04·2	5:07·2	5:10·2	5:13·2	5:19·2	5:28·2	5:43·2

SHORT COURSE METRES

	−5%	−3%	−2%	−1%	**National Standard**	+1%	+2%	+3%	+4%	+5%	+7%	+10%	+15%
100 free	52·6	53·6	54·1	54·6	**55·1**	55·6	56·1	56·6	57·1	57·6	58·6	1:00·1	1:02·6
200 free	1:53·4	1:55·8	1:57·0	1:58·2	**1:59·4**	2:00·6	2:01·8	2:03·0	2:04·2	2:05·4	2:07·8	2:11·4	2:17·4
400 free	4:00·0	4:05·0	4:07·5	4:10·0	**4:12·5**	4:15·0	4:17·5	4:20·0	4:22·5	4:25·0	4:30·0	4:37·5	4:50·0
800 free	8:23·4	8:34·0	8:39·3	8:44·6	**8:49·9**	8:55·2	9:00·5	9:05·8	9:11·1	9:16·5	9:27·1	9:43·0	10:09·5
1500 free	15:50·8	16:10·8	18:20·8	16:30·8	**16:40·8**	16:50·8	17:00·8	17:10·8	17:20·8	17:30·8	17:50·8	18:20·8	19:10·8
100 back	1:00·4	1:01·6	1:02·2	1:02·8	**1:03·4**	1:04·0	1:04·6	1:05·2	1:05·8	1:06·4	1:07·6	1:09·4	1:12·4
200 back	2:11·9	2:14·6	2:16·0	2:17·4	**2:18·8**	2:20·2	2:21·6	2:22·9	2:24·4	2:25·7	2:28·5	2:32·7	2:39·6
100 breast	1:07·4	1:08·8	1:09·5	1:10·1	**1:10·9**	1:11·6	1:12·3	1:13·0	1:13·7	1:14·4	1:15·8	1:17·9	1:21·5
200 breast	2:27·3	2:30·3	2:31·8	2:33·3	**2:34·8**	2:36·3	2:37·8	2:39·3	2:40·8	2:42·3	2:45·3	2:49·8	2:57·3
100 fly	57·1	58·7	59·3	59·9	**1:00·5**	1:01·1	1:01·7	1:02·3	1:02·9	1:03·5	1:04·7	1:06·5	1:09·5
200 fly	2:07·4	2:10·0	2:11·3	2:12·5	**2:13·7**	2:15·0	2:16·3	2:17·6	2:18·9	2:20·2	2:22·8	2:26·7	2:33·2
200 im	2:09·5	2:12·2	2:13·6	2:14·9	**2:16·3**	2:17·7	2:19·0	2:20·4	2:21·8	2:23·1	2:25·8	2:29·9	2:36·7
400 im	4:37·4	4:43·2	4:46·1	4:49·0	**4:51·9**	4:54·8	4:57·7	5:00·6	5:03·5	5:06·4	5:12·2	5:20·9	5:35·4

COMPARATIVE PERCENTAGE CHART WOMEN (Canada 1976)

LONG COURSE METRES

	−5%	−3%	−2%	−1%	National Standard	+1%	+2%	+3%	+4%	+5%	+7%	+10%	+15%
100 free	58·8	1:00·0	1:00·6	1:01·2	**1:01·88**	1:02·5	1:03·1	1:03·7	1:04·3	1:05·0	1:06·2	1:08·0	1:11·2
200 free	2:05·6	2:08·2	2:09·5	2:10·9	**2:12·02**	2:13·5	2:14·8	2:16·1	2:17·5	2:18·8	2:21·4	2:25·4	2:32·0
400 free	4:22·0	4:24·8	4:30·3	4:33·1	**4:35·77**	4:38·5	4:41·3	4:44·0	4:46·8	4:49·6	4:55·1	5:03·3	5:17·7
800 free	8:55·4	9:07·0	9:12·8	9:18·6	**9:27·46**	9:33·2	9:39·0	9:44·8	9:50·6	9:56·4	10:08·0	10:25·4	10:54·4
1500 free	16:58·5	17:19·9	17:30·6	17:41·3	**17:55·0**	18:05·7	18:26·4	18:37·3	18:48·0	18:58·7	19:20·1	19:52·2	20:45·7
100 back	1:07·4	1:08·8	1:09·5	1:10·7	**1:10·88**	1:11·6	1:12·3	1:13·0	1:13·7	1:14·4	1:15·8	1:17·9	1:21·5
200 back	2:25·2	2:28·2	2:29·7	2:31·3	**2:32·78**	2:34·3	2:35·8	2:37·3	2:38·9	2:40·4	2:43·5	2:48·0	2:55·7
100 breast	1:17·2	1:19·4	1:20·1	1:20·8	**1:21·53**	1:22·3	1:23·1	1:23·9	1:24·7	1:25·5	1:27·0	1:29·2	1:32·9
200 breast	2:45·8	2:49·2	2:50·9	2:52·6	**2:54·33**	2:56·0	2:57·7	2:59·4	3:01·1	3:02·8	3:06·2	3:11·3	3:19·8
100 fly	1:05·3	1:06·6	1:07·3	1:08·0	**1:08·61**	1:09·3	1:10·0	1:10·7	1:11·4	1:12·1	1:13·5	1:15·5	1:19·0
200 fly	2:22·7	2:25·7	2:27·2	2:28·7	**2:30·15**	2:31·7	2:33·2	2:35·0	2:36·2	2:37·7	2:40·7	2:45·2	2:52·7
200 im	2:25·1	2:28·1	2:29·6	2:31·2	**2:32·70**	2:34·2	2:35·8	2:37·3	2:38·8	2:40·3	2:43·3	2:47·9	2:55·6
400 im	5:04·3	5:10·7	5:13·9	5:17·1	**5:20·35**	5:23·5	5:26·7	5:29·9	5:33·1	5:36·3	5:42·7	5:52·3	6:08·3

SHORT COURSE METRES

	−5%	−3%	−2%	−1%	National Standard	+1%	+2%	+3%	+4%	+5%	+7%	+10%	+15%
100 free	57·2	58·4	59·0	59·6	**1:00·2**	1:00·8	1:01·4	1:02·0	1:02·6	1:03·2	1:04·4	1:06·2	1:09·2
200 free	2:02·4	2:04·9	2:06·2	2:07·5	**2:08·8**	2:10·1	2:11·3	2:12·6	2:13·9	2:17·8	2:17·8	2:21·7	2:28·1
400 free	4:15·6	4:20·9	4:23·6	4:26·3	**4:29·0**	4:31·7	4:34·8	4:37·0	4:39·7	4:42·4	4:47·8	4:55·9	5:09·3
800 free	8:46·6	8:57·6	9:03·1	9:08·6	**9:14·1**	9:19·6	9:25·1	9:30·6	9:36·1	9:41·6	9:52·6	10:09·1	10:36·6
1500 free	16:36·9	16:57·9	17:08·4	17:18·9	**17:29·4**	17:39·9	17:50·4	18:00·8	18:11·5	18:22·2	18:43·2	19:14·7	20:07·2
100 back	1:06·2	1:07·6	1:08·3	1:09·0	**1:09·7**	1:10·4	1:11·1	1:11·8	1:12·5	1:13·2	1:14·6	1:16·6	1:20·1
200 back	2:22·9	2:25·9	2:27·4	2:28·9	**2:30·4**	2:31·9	2:33·4	2:34·9	2:36·4	2:37·9	2:40·9	2:45·4	2:52·9
100 breast	1:15·3	1:17·1	1:17·9	1:18·7	**1:19·5**	1:20·3	1:21·1	1:21·9	1:22·7	1:23·5	1:25·1	1:27·5	1:31·5
200 breast	2:41·3	2:45·2	2:46·9	2:48·6	**2:50·3**	2:52·0	2:53·7	2:55·3	2:57·0	2:58·8	3:02·2	3:07·3	3:15·8
100 fly	1:03·9	1:05·3	1:05·9	1:06·6	**1:07·3**	1:07·9	1:08·6	1:09·3	1:10·0	1:10·7	1:12·5	1:14·0	1:17·4
200 fly	2:20·0	2:22·9	2:24·4	2:25·9	**2:27·4**	2:28·8	2:30·3	2:31·8	2:33·3	2:34·7	2:37·7	2:42·1	2:49·5
200 im	2:22·0	2:25·0	2:26·5	2:28·0	**2:29·5**	2:31·0	2:32·5	2:34·0	2:35·5	2:37·0	2:39·9	2:44·4	2:51·9
400 im	4:58·3	5:04·6	5:07·7	5:10·8	**5:14·0**	5:17·1	5:20·3	5:23·4	5:26·5	5:29·7	5:36·0	5:45·4	6:01·1

Afternoon Programme, Tuesday and Thursday

1. 15 × 50 metres breaststroke departing every 50 seconds.
2. 15 × 50 metres backstroke sprints departing every 45 seconds.
3. 15 × 50 metres freestyle legs tied sprints departing every 40 seconds.
4. 15 × 50 metres freestyle sprints departing every 35 seconds. This will be the first time you have attempted working at this high point. Do not swim 34 seconds for each sprint thereby making it virtually one long non-stop swim. Aim for 31 seconds with 4 seconds rest.
5. 40 × 25 butterfly sprints departing every 25 seconds. Since we only have the pool for an hour this will be a good test as to your potential.

Afternoon total—4,000 metres
Weekly total—61,300 yards
Allotted grand total—122,600 yards.
Your personal grand total—. . . . .

Work Sheet No. 3. Confidential

September 29, 1975.

Dear Swimmers,

Average mileage was up last week with five swimmers reaching the target. Main weakness was the kicking section. Congratulations to Paula who swam 4·06 for four of the 4 × 100s on the 1 min. 20 secs. It seems that we are developing into endurance types more so than sprinters, so we will have one session this week to test out your distance potential. I will try your endurance against that of three Australian distance champions I have coached, Stephen Holland, Brad Cooper and Debbie Palmer. You will not be able to repeat their times at this stage, but I will ask you for a 100 per cent effort and we will compare times. Canada has never produced a great distance star, either male or female, so we will investigate this weakness. The Canadian Olympic selection times of 9:11·2 for the girls' 800 metres freestyle (short course) and 16:40·2 for the mens' 1,500 metres freestyle (short course) and 16:40·2 for the mens' 1,500 metres freestyle (short course) seem to be the easiest ways to make the team. Listed below are the best training times of Olympians Holland, Cooper and Palmer. Record your times in the columns provided and we will compare.

For training this week we will repeat week No. 2 with the addition of the special Saturday afternoon session for the distance swimmers.

Weekly total—61,300 yards
Allotted grand total—183,900 yards
Your personal grand total—. . . . .

15 × 100 metres sprints on the 1 minute 20 seconds

Brad Cooper	Steve Holland	Debbie Palmer	Alan	Bill	Paula	Metres
60·0	60·1	66·0				100
60·9	62·1	67·0				200
61·6	62·5	67·7				300
62·9	62·4	67·0				400
62·7	62·6	67·4				500
63·6	62·9	66·7				600
63·9	63·7	66·1				700
64·3	63·2	66·1				800
64·0	63·6					900
64·1	63·2					1,000
64·0	62·9					1,100
64·2	62·6					1,200
64·0	62·5					1,300
64·1	62·0					1,400
62·9	61·1					1,500
15m. 47.2s. Jan. '73	15m. 37.4s. Feb. '73	8m. 54.0s. Mar. '73				

Work Sheet No. 4. Confidential

October 6, 1975.

Dear Swimmers,

You are now getting on top of the programme. Last week was a good one. Your repeats were much more even and your kicking improved. We will work very hard on Monday, Tuesday, Wednesday and Thursday. Friday will be a rest day. We will train on Saturday morning. Sunday is our first swim meet of the season and although our mileage is not high yet, I want a good showing from you. First of all I want to see how you perform in competition and also assess the level of your fitness.

Paula, your time of 9 minutes 21 seconds, for the broken 800 metres was respectable. Bill, your time of 17 minutes 21·4 seconds shows that you have a long way to go before you are a Stephen Holland. Alan, I was moderately satisfied with your 16 minutes 58·6 seconds. I am sending you to Dr. —— to see what can be done about your shoulder soreness. Ken, you must pay more attention to your breaststroke kick, you are getting a good whipping action but you are not drawing your heels up tight enough on to your buttocks. Chuck, swimming with your legs tied will increase the strength in your backstroke, as long as you do not overdo it. Put your leg tie band on as often as you like especially in the 100s and 50s.

There are no local fresh fruits or vegetables during the long Canadian winter so I will now ask you to take a few supplementary vitamins each day. I will see you all individually regarding this. This week we are scheduling 65,000 yards. Here is your programme.

Morning Programme, Monday and Wednesday

1. 500 yards S.K.P. on freestyle.
2. 1,000 yards backstroke with legs tied and using hand paddles.
3. 500 yards breaststroke in less than 7 minutes.
4. 10 × 100 yards sprints departing every 1 min. 30 secs. (freestylers aim for 62 seconds).
5. 10 × 100 yards sprints departing every 1 min. 20 secs. (aim for 61 secs.).
6. 10 × 100 yards sprints departing every 1 min. 10 secs. (aim for less than 60 secs. as often as possible). This is to be a superior quality section.
7. 1,000 yards fast kick with flippers (less than 13 minutes). Freestyle, backstroke or dolphin.
8. 500 yards non-stop butterfly with very little pressure but working on technique.
9. 20 × 25 yards butterfly sprints departing every 30 seconds and breathing every third stroke.

Morning total—7,000 yards.

Afternoon Programme, Monday and Wednesday

1. 500 metres S.K.P. on breaststroke.
2. 10 × 300 metres freestyle departing every 3 mins. 45 secs. Form strokers have to do 250 metres departing every 3 mins. 45 secs. straight behind the freestylers.
3. 500 metres backstroke for technique and tumbles.
4. 60 × 50 metres sprints with legs tied and using hand paddles departing every 45 seconds. Have a short break at 30 repeats. If your shoulders start to pain let me know immediately.
5. 1,000 metres I.M. non-stop.

Afternoon total—8,000 metres.

Morning Programme, Tuesday, Thursday and Saturday

1. 500 yards I.M. as a loosen up.
2. 5 × 800 yards efforts with 30 seconds rests between each (one of these efforts to be on your secondary stroke or an I.M.).
3. 5 × 200 yards I.M. departing every 3 minutes and working hard on your best strokes, concentrating on technique on your poorer strokes.
4. 20 × 25 yards sprints on the 40 seconds (no breathers).
5. 1,000 yards backstroke with hand paddles concentrating on minimum body roll and a hard push down at the end of the stroke.
6. 1,000 yards very fast flipper kick. Breaststrokers to do breaststroke kick with board.

Morning total—8,000 yards.

Afternoon Programme, Tuesday

1. Try for 4,500 metres in one hour. Start off gradually and build up speed. If you wish to change strokes you can only do it after 1,000 metres.

Afternoon Programme, Thursday

1. 4,000 metres I.M. in the 60 minutes allotted pool time.
Afternoon total—8,500 metres.
Weekly total—65,000 yards.
Allotted grand total—248,900 yards.
Your personal grand total—. . . . .

Work Sheet No. 5. Confidential

October 13, 1975

Dear Swimmers,

Congratulations, last week's work was a big forward step in quality. I was particularly pleased with your performances at the Windsor meet. Attached is a cutting from the local paper. I want you to start scrap books and this cutting will be your first entry. The best individual swims were:

* Paula's 100 yards freestyle in 56·6 seconds, because you worked on style all the way;

* Kathy's 200 yards backstroke in 2 mins. 19·2 secs., a big improvement on your previous best;

* Chuck's 200 yards backstroke in 2 mins 8·7 secs., a fine performance especially as your training is limited by your studies;

* Alan's 200 yards I.M. in 2 mins. 8·4 secs., showed up the weakness in your breaststroke, the other strokes were excellent;

* Bill's 100 yards freestyle in 53·2 seconds, makes you the best sprinter in the London "Y", but we still have ten yards to go to reach world class; My thanks to you all for working the relays like true champions.

It is obvious from talking with the coaches at Windsor that there are no teams in Canada exceeding 80,000 yards a week, very few seem to be passing 50,000 yards weekly. We will make 80,000 yards our target but you are not quite ready to lift up to this level yet and still maintain the highest quality. Here is our new schedule for 70,000 yards.

Morning Programme, Wednesday and Friday

1. 1,500 yards freestyle starting out steadily and building up speed as you go. Try to make each 200 yards a negative split.
2. 1,500 yards with legs tied and hand paddles (freestyle or backstroke). Make this and 85% effort timed.
3. 15 × 100 yards freestyle departing every 1 min. 20 secs. and aiming for an average of 61 seconds.
4. 1,500 yards kicking with flippers and board in less than 20 minutes.
5. 1,000 yards stretching out on any stroke except freestyle.

Morning total—7,000 yards

Afternoon Programme, Monday, Wednesday and Friday

1. 5 × 100 metres I.M. departing every 1 min. 30 secs. as a warm up.

2. 500 metres breaststroke kick under 8 mins. 45 secs.
3. 500 metres backstroke with the legs tied.
4. 10 × 200 metres (broken with 5 seconds rest at each 50). Aim to better or equal your best straight time for the distance.
5. 500 metres fast dolphin kick with flippers. Ken and Alan, do breaststroke kick on board instead.
6. 10 × 200 metres on your major stroke departing every 3 mins. 30 secs. for form strokers and every 3 minutes for freestylers. Get within 10 seconds of your best time by doing negative splits throughout.
7. 40 × 25 metres sprints in sets of ten in the medley order of strokes departing every 30 seconds.
Afternoon total—7,000 metres

Morning Programme, Tuesday, Thursday and Saturday

1. 5 × 400 yards I.M. departing every 6 minutes.
2. 5 × 400 yards freestyle with the legs tied and using hand paddles, departing every 6 minutes (Chuck and Kathy to do backstroke).
3. 5 × 400 yards freestyle departing every 5 mins. 30 secs. Girls aim for 4 mins. 20 secs., boys aim for 4 mins. 10 secs. or better.
Morning total—6,000 yards

Afternoon Programme, Tuesday and Thursday

1. 20 × 25 metres butterfly sprints departing every 25 seconds.
2. 20 × 25 metres breaststroke sprints departing every 30 seconds.
3. 20 × 25 metres backstroke sprints departing every 25 seconds.
4. 20 × 25 metres freestyle sprints departing every 20 seconds.
5. 1,500 metres with hand paddles. Ken to do breaststroke, Paula and Chuck to do backstroke, Bill and Paula to try butterfly, Alan not to use paddles at all.
6. 200 metres of free choice as a loosen down.
Afternoon total—3,700 metres
Weekly total—70,240 yards
Allotted grand total—329,140 yards
Your personal grand total—. . . . .

Work Sheet No. 6. Confidential

October 20, 1975

Dear Swimmers,
The good news this week is that we have made worthwhile contact with Dr. . . . . . . who seems genuinely interested in our work. He is an old swimmer himself. Dr. . . . . . . phoned me about Alan's sore shoulders and explained that there are several ways to prevent "swimmers' shoulder" and several ways of repairing them, but it takes time and care to do so.

He suggested that most coaches are in error when they apply heat to the deltoids. The treatment that he recommends is to ice the affected area before training commences. This is the best way to increase the local circulation. If you have any shoulder soreness at all I want you to keep a supply of Styro foam cups of ice in your freezer at home. On leaving home take one of the cups with you and, whilst in the car, ice your arm on and around the region of soreness until it is quite numb and very red. You should do this for about ten minutes by using a circular movement. As the ice melts down break down the sides of the cup. Here is an extract of the doctor's report:

> Examination reveals no wasting of the deltoid by any means. He has exquisite tenderness right over the supraspinatous tendon and this can be brought into view by internally rotating his arm and putting straight downward pressure. He has no weakness. Forced abduction causes him pain.
>
> This is a classical case of supraspinatous tendonitis in a swimmer or so-called "swimmer's shoulder". He has a big meet this week-end and accordingly since he is training down, anyway we have asked that he stay off doing excessive arms and carry on with the icing. We have put him on high doses of Phenylbutazone for a couple of days and then tapered him on down. When he starts into training again if he has exacerbation of his symptoms, we should get him on a therapeutic programme at the University. Thank you for having me see this patient.

If this treatment is not successful we must consider Cortizone injections but this is usually a drastic move. At the first indications of "swimmer's shoulder" you must not use paddles, swim with your legs tied, pull a buoy, or swim constantly on the one stroke. Your training sessions should not be as long as usual because it is the constant repetitive movement that inflames the tendon.

For training this week we will repeat last week's schedule. As you know, Chuck and Alan did not manage to do the full workout last week. This will be a supreme effort for all to reach the target before we move on to better things.

Weekly total—70,240 yards
Allotted grand total—399,380 yards
Your personal grand total— . . . .

Work Sheet No. 7. Confidential

October 27, 1975

Dear Swimmers,

Next Sunday I have arranged for sanctioned time trials to be held. The main purpose behind the trials will be to break several Ontario records, in the relays. They have not been bettered for some time and are not particularly hard to break. Still, the more records we can break, the more times our names appear in the record book, the more attention the C.A.S.A. officials will give us. Herewith, I have drawn a rough graph of the yardage you have been alloted compared with the actual yardage you have covered since we started this special project. If we do not do this type of exercise often we are apt to fall into a very common trap, that is, thinking that as a team we are doing more yardage than we actually are.

In Australia and the United States there is a standard often used to assess the endurance of first class swimmers. Many clubs strike a special badge for the performance I am about to convey to you. Shane Gould and Stephen Holland are the two superstars who did best in this test in Australia. The test is to swim 200 lengths of a 25 metres pool in sixty minutes. Since we only have one hour allotted pool time on Tuesday night I will put you through this test then. It is not an easy task and of course it will have to be freestyle all the way.

We are lifting to new levels this week—73,000 yards. Good luck.

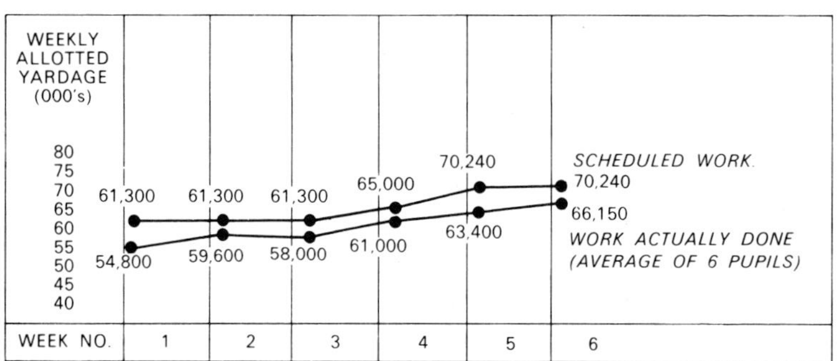

Morning Programme, Monday, Wednesday and Friday

1. 1,000 yards of fast kick with flippers on your special stroke in less than 14 minutes. Ken to do breaststroke kick without flippers.
2. 10 × 200 yards of legs tied with hand paddles departing every 3 minutes on your main strokes.
3. 1,000 yards of alternative backstroke and breaststroke 50s. This is for technique more than speed.
4. 10 × 200 yards freestyle sprints in a descending order departing every 3 mins. 30 secs. 2:15, 2:15, 2:12, 2:12, 2:10, 2:10, 2:08, 2:08, 2:06, 2:03.
5. 10 × 100 yards I.M. on the 1 min. 30 secs. (Paula do 'fly, Ken try for breaststroke, others do I.M.).
6. 20 × 25 yards of your own choice departing every 30 seconds.

Morning total—7,500 yards

Afternoon Programme, Monday, Wednesday and Friday

This type of programme places emphasis on your ability to stress yourself in increasing doses.

1. 40 × 25 metres sprints on the 25 seconds (any stroke).
2. 500 metres backstroke thinking about your catch, I prefer a deep one.
3. 20 × 50 metres sprints on the 45 seconds (any strokes).
4. 500 metres breaststroke with tumble turns.
4. 500 metres breaststroke with tumble turns.
5. 10 × 100 metres freestyle or I.M. departing every 1 min. 25 secs.
6. 500 metres I.M.
7. 5 × 200 metres freestyle departing every 2 min. 45 secs.
8. 500 metres butterfly non-stop with tumble turns.

Note that as your sprint sections progress you are getting less rest.
Afternoon total—6,000 metres

Morning Programme, Tuesday, Thursday and Saturday

1. 500 yards S.K.P. on breaststroke.
2. 500 yards S.K.P. on backstroke.
3. 3,000 yards fast swimming on your main stroke in less than:
   freestyle—34 minutes;
   butterfly—38 minutes;
   backstroke—38 minutes;
   breaststroke—40 minutes.
4. 500 yards of fast freestyle or dolphin kick.
5. 40 × 50 yards sprints, the first 20 on the 40 seconds, the second 20 on the 35 seconds.
6. 500 yards of your choice but it must be something that you need to improve.

Morning total—7,000 yards

Afternoon Programme, Tuesday

1. A special attempt to swim 5,000 metres in 60 minutes. I will provide "counters" to check on your laps. You will start on the whistle and stop on the bell. I will record your effort in next week's news sheet.

Afternoon Programme, Thursday

We will work on swim drills for the medley. To complete the 4,000 metres in one hour is a world class performance. See how you rate.

1. 1,000 metres breaststroke fast with correct touch turns.
2. 1,000 metres backstroke with the legs tied.
3. 1,000 metres butterfly breathing every two strokes.
4. 1,000 metres freestyle with hand paddles.

Afternoon total—9,000 metres.
Weekly total—73,200 yards
Allotted grand total—472,580 yards
Your personal grand total—. . . . .

Work Sheet No. 8. Confidential

November 3, 1975

Dear Swimmers,
Since we all failed on our Tuesday afternoon test we will repeat it again in one month. I have recorded your lengths for reference.
Bill Young, 198 lengths
Paula Parris, 195 lengths
Kathy Becker, 189 lengths
Ken Fitzpatrick, 184 lengths
Alan Webster, sore shoulders
Chuck Grace, absent

I have attached the results of the time trials. Place this cutting in your log book. We now hold three national relay records and seven Ontario relay records.

We are repeating last week's schedule, mainly because there were a few absentees (school exams) and because it is a high quality programme. The only alteration will be on Tuesday afternoon when you will be allowed to make up your own programme to total 4,000 metres. I will leave it to you to arrange a schedule based on your needs.

Weekly total—72,100 yards
Allotted grand total—544,680 yards
Your personal grand total—. . . . .

Work Sheet No. 9. Confidential

November 10, 1975

Dear Swimmers,
Because you are all starting to look a little weary I am going to ease back the yardage and the efforts this week. Most of the work will be on drills and rather time consuming. You may come to the pool at 6 a.m. instead of 5:40 a.m. and you can have Tuesday and Thursday afternoons off to catch up on studies. The only real efforts for the week will be a timed circuit over 3,000 metres and one over 6,000 metres. Make the most of this easy week by not exhausting yourselves on other sports or school physical activities. Congratulations on passing the half million yards mark in eight weeks. This is approximately 284 miles. A very good effort. You can have a full day off training when we reach one million yards.

Morning Programme, Monday, Wednesday and Friday

1. 500 yards freestyle breathing on the left side and using the left arm only.

2. 500 yards freestyle breathing on the right side and using the right arm only.
3. 500 yards backstroke using the left arm only with a hand paddle.
4. 500 yards backstroke using the right arm only with a hand paddle.
5. 1,000 yards dolphin kick with flippers and kick board.
6. 500 yards breaststroke.
7. 500 yards butterfly.
8. 1,000 yards I.M.
Morning total—5,000 yards

Afternoon Programme, Monday

A timed circuit over 6,000 metres swimming in this order:
1,000 metres breaststroke
1,000 metres backstroke.
1,000 metres freestyle with legs tied.
1,000 metres freestyle.
1,000 metres I.M.
40 × 25 metres butterfly sprints departing every 25 seconds.
This will be non-stop, timed and recorded.

Afternoon Programme, Wednesday

1. 5 × 400 metres I.M. departing every 7 minutes.
2. 5 × 200 metres I.M. departing every 3 mins. 30 secs.
3. 10 × 100 metres I.M. departing every 1 min. 45 secs.
4. 1,000 metres of your choice.

Afternoon Programme, Friday

1. 500 metres of polo swimming, i.e. freestyle with the head held very high and looking straight ahead.
2. 500 metres pectoral pulling.
3. A timed circuit over 3,000 metres swimming in this order:
500 metres breaststroke.
500 metres backstroke.
500 metres butterfly.
500 metres freestyle.
500 metres freestyle with legs tied.
500 metres I.M.
This will be non-stop, timed and recorded
Afternoon total—15,000 metres

Morning Programme Tuesday, Thursday and Saturday

1. 500 yards breaststroke kick with a board.
2. 500 yards breaststroke pull, refrain from doing exaggerated dolphin kick.
3. 500 yards stretch-out breaststroke.
4. 500 yards backstroke kick with arms extended overhead.
5. 500 yards backstroke with legs tied.
5. 500 yards backstroke with legs tied.

6. 500 yards backstroke stretch-out.
7. 500 yards dolphin kick with board.
8. 500 yards butterfly pulling a buoy.
9. 500 yards butterfly.
10. 500 yards freestyle for technique.

Morning total—5,000 yards
Weekly total—46,500 yards
Allotted grand total—591,180 yards
Your personal grand total—. . . . .

Work Sheet No. 10. Confidential

November 17, 1975

Dear Swimmers,

This week will be the last before we alter the system. The quality so far has been good but after this week we will start again on low yardage and build-up to higher levels. But, the quality will be the very best I feel you can manage at your stage of development. Each ten weeks we will step up in quality similar to the East German swimmers. Next week I will introduce land exercises but these will be done on the deck because home exercising systems are not very reliable.

Several swimmers (Kathryn Irvine, Jane Thompson, Leonard Gushe, John Dawdy, Peter Gauld and Dick Treleaven) are all showing potential and are training well enough to be considered for our special squad. So, at the end of week twenty we will probably reselect and enlarge the experimental squad to ten members.

Here are the results of the timed circuits. Place your time in your log book.

6,000 metres timed circuit

Ken Fitzpatrick—1 hr. 36 mins. 10 secs.
Alan Webster —1 hr. 37 mins.
Paula Parris —1 hr. 39 mins. 15 secs.
Chuck Grace —1 hr. 39 mins. 22 secs.
Bill Young —1 hr. 39 mins. 25 secs.
Kathy Becker —absent

3,000 metres timed circuit

Bill Young —44 mins. 58 secs.
Ken Fitzpatrick—45 mins. 48 secs.
Kathy Becker —45 mins. 53 secs.
Paula Parris —46 mins. 20 secs.
Chuck Grace —46 mins. 26 secs.
Alan Webster —absent

Faster times are expected when we repeat these circuits in December. Our aim this week is to reach 75,000 yards, surely an Ontario record for an Age Group team.

Morning Programme, Monday, Wednesday and Friday

1. 3,000 yards freestyle with alternate 500 yards of steady and fast swimming throughout.
2. 2,000 yards non-stop I.M.
3. 1,000 yards fast kicking either freestyle or dolphin, with flippers and board.
4. 40 × 50 yards sprints: 10 breaststroke on 50 seconds
10 backstroke on 45 seconds
10 butterfly on 40 seconds
10 freestyle on 35 seconds.

Morning total—8,000 yards

Afternoon Programme, Monday, Wednesday and Friday

1. 1,000 metres S.K.P. freestyle.
2. 2,000 metres of alternate freestyle and backstroke 50s with hand paddles.
3. 1,000 metres butterfly pulling a float.
4. 1,000 metres breaststroke breathing every stroke for the down 25s and breathing every 2 strokes for the up 25s throughout.
5. 1,000 metres of free choice with equipment.

Afternoon total—6,000 metres

Morning Programme, Tuesday, Thursday and Saturday

1. 3 × 1,500 yards freestyle at 90%, 85%, 90% (negative splits). Take I minute rests between the efforts.
2. 1,000 yards breaststroke with hand paddles (small) concentrating on the lifted elbows and the recovery.
3. 500 yards left arm backstroke with hand paddle.
4. 500 yards right arm backstroke with hand paddle.
5. 30 × 50 yards on your stroke at 90% with 5 seconds rest between.

Morning total—8,000 yards

Afternoon Programme, Tuesday and Thursday

1. 70 × 50 metres sprints departing every 40 seconds. Place paddles by poolside and use them anytime throughout.

Afternoon total—3,500 metres
Weekly total—75,500 yards
Allotted grand total—666,680 yards
Your personal grand total— . . . .

Work Sheet No. 11. Confidential

November 24, 1975

Dear Swimmers,

We are now about to embark on a whole new way of training. On Monday morning I will explain the importance of quality, the intelligent approach, how you must start to think for your self, assess your own work as you speed along. The champions, I mean the really great champions, are not swimmers who arrive at the Olympics by hard work alone. It now requires science and superior intelligence to become the best in the world. This is what we will be seeking.

First of all, you should know that the system we are about to undertake has been used before with success. I will give you the details briefly so that you can have faith in our plans.

* In 1962 I selected ten swimmers who showed potential, to form a special squad. Their target was the 1964 Olympics. At a meeting I explained our purpose, outlined how hard it would be and presented them with target sheets for the next two years. For various reasons four swimmers proved unsuitable. Of the remaining six, five trained well enough to gain selection for the Olympics.
* In 1966 six pupils were selected from the squad to train for the Olympics at Mexico City. Five of these pupils gained selection. So you see, the chances of success are fairly high. It is up to you to keep ahead of the quarterly target times that I am setting you. We are planning for the Commonwealth Games in 1978. The qualifying times are graduated evenly so if you fall behind we will analyse the reasons. If you are ahead, stay that way by greater determination and dedication to the task. There will be rewards along the way, no doubt because you are quality swimmers and the times I have set you are first class.
* In 1972, two out of three pupils successfully followed the system and made the Olympics at Munich.

Here now is a table on which I have based your target times for the Commonwealth Games of 1978 and the Olympics of 1980 (freestyle this month, form strokes next month).

We will now specialise. Sprinters will have their own schedule and work in lane 2. Distance swimmers will be in lane 1. You will have one programme for the weekday mornings and one for the afternoons. To break the monotony we will reverse the schedules each day, that is, working down the programme one day and up the programme the next.

Sprinters' Morning Programme, Monday through Saturday

1. 500 yards S.K.P. on freestyle.
2. 10 × 100 yards freestyle departing every 1 min. 30 secs. and holding steady at 63 seconds each sprint.
3. 5 × 100 yards freestyle departing every 1 min. 30 secs. and averaging 61 seconds each sprint.
4. 5 × 100 yards freestyle departing every 2 minutes and aiming for 59 seconds each sprint.

LONG COURSE METRES (FREESTYLE)
QUARTERLY TARGET TIMES

	100	200	400	800 / 1500		100	200	400	800 / 1500	M	Y
Olympic Trials Times 1976, Montreal	56·4	2:1·5	4:18	17:06	M	56·4	2:01·5	4:18·0	17:06·0	J	1976
	61·6	2:10·5	4:34·7	9:24	F	61·6	2:10·5	4:34·7	9:24·0	J	1976
					M	59·5	2:12·0	4:29·0	17:50·0	S	1976
					F	64·5	2:22·0	4:45·0	9:38·0	S	1976
					M	59·0	2:10·0	4:26·0	17:40·0	D	1976
					F	64·0	2:20·0	4:42·0	9:33·0	D	1976
					M	58·5	2:08·0	4:23·0	17:30·0	M	1977
					F	63·5	2:18·0	4:38·0	9:28·0	M	1977
					M	58·0	2:06·0	4:20·0	17:20·0	J	1977
					F	63·0	2:16·0	4:35·0	9:23·0	J	1977
					M	57·5	2:04·0	4:17·0	17:10·0	S	1977
					F	62·0	2:14·0	4:32·0	9:18·0	S	1977
					M	57·0	2:02·0	4:14·0	17:00·0	D	1977
Predicted Trials Times					F	61·0	2:12·0	4:29·0	9:13·0	D	1977
					M	56·3	2:00·0	4:11·0	16:50·0	M	1978
					F	60·0	2:10·0	4:26·0	9:08·0	M	1978
1978,	55·3	1:58	4:08	16:40	M	55·3	1:58·0	4:08·0	16:40·0	J	1978
Edmonton	59·0	2:08	4:23	9:03	F	59·0	2:08·0	4:23·0	9:03·0	J	1978
					M	56·5	2:05·0	4:12·0	16:30·0	S	1978
					F	61·0	2:15·0	4:31·0	9:20·0	S	1978
					M	56·0	2:03·5	4:10·0	16:25·5	D	1978
					F	60·5	2:13·5	4:29·0	9:15·0	D	1978
					M	55·5	2:02·0	4:08·0	16:20·0	M	1979
					F	60·0	2:12·0	4:27·0	9:10·0	M	1979
					M	55·0	2:00·5	4:06·0	16:15·0	J	1979
					F	59·5	2:10·5	4:25·0	9:05·0	J	1979
Predicted Olympic Trial Times					M	54·4	1:59·0	4:04·0	16:10·0	S	1979
					F	59·0	2:09·0	4:23·0	9:00·0	S	1979
					M	54·0	1:57·5	4:02·0	16:05·0	D	1979
					F	58·5	2:07·5	4:21·0	8:55·0	D	1979
1980,	53·5	1:56	4:00	16:00	M	53·5	1:56·0	4:00·0	16:00·0	M	1980
Moscow	58·0	2:06	4:19	8:51	F	58·0	2:06·0	4:19·0	8:50·0	M	1980

5. 10 × 25 yards freestyle departing every 30 seconds, target time 12·5 seconds.
6. 10 × 25 yards freestyle departing every 30 seconds, target time 12·0 seconds.
7. 15 × 100 yards freestyle or backstroke with hand paddles and the legs tied departing every 1 min. 45 secs. and working at 90%.
Morning total—4,500 yards

Sprinters' Afternoon Programme, Monday, Wednesday and Friday

1. 500 metres backstroke with a very long and steady stroke (push right through).
2. 500 metres backstroke gliding and tumble turns.
3. 10 × 50 metres sprints departing every 60 seconds and averaging 29 seconds from push-off. "Fliers aim for 32s backstrokers 34s, breast-strokers 37s. If unable to maintain the speed extend rest intervals out to 90 seconds.
4. 10 × 50 metres sprints departing every 55 seconds and freestylers averaging 30 seconds, etc.
5. 10 × 50 metres sprints departing every 50 seconds and freestylers averaging 31 seconds, etc.

6. 10 × 50 metres sprints departing every 45 seconds and freestylers averaging 32 seconds, etc.
7. 20 × 25 metres sprints departing every 40 seconds and freestylers aiming for 12·5 seconds.
8. 15 × 100 metres with paddles departing every 1 min. 30 secs. and working at 90% on your main stroke.
9. 15 × 100 flipper kick sprints departing every 1 min. 30 secs. all to be under 1 min. 10 secs.
Afternoon total—6,500 metres

Sprinters' Afternoon Programme, Tuesday and Thursday

1. 20 × 25 metres freestyle kick sprints departing every 35 seconds.
2. 500 metres freestyle correcting your main fault.
3. 20 × 25 metres freestyle or backstroke sprints with legs tied departing every 40 seconds.
4. 500 metres backstroke.
5. 20 × 25 metres freestyle or backstroke sprints departing every 30 seconds.
6. 500 metres dolphin or breaststroke kick with a board.
7. 40 × 25 metres butterfly sprints departing every 30 seconds. (Try to get as many of the sprints done before the 6 p.m. whistle).
Afternoon total—4,000 metres

Middle Distance Swimmers' Morning Programme, Monday through Saturday

1. 500 yards freestyle S.K.P.
2. 1,500 yards freestyle with hand paddles and legs tied as an 85% effort.
3. 5 × 400 yards efforts departing every 5 mins. 30 secs. and holding steady at best time plus 15 seconds. Do these as negative splits.
4. 20 × 25 yards butterfly or backstroke sprints on the 25 seconds.
5. 20 × 100 yards sprints at absolute steady speed, try for 64 seconds, departing every 1 min. 15 secs.
6. 15 × 100 yards flipper kick sprints departing every 1 min. 30 secs., all to be under 1 min. 10 secs.
Morning total—8,000 yards

Middle Distance Swimmers' Afternoon Programme, Monday, Wednesday and Friday

1. 500 metres loosen up with super long push back stroke.
2. 15 × 100 metres working at 90% effort but with only 5 seconds rest intervals.
3. 15 × 100 metres legs tied sprints working at 90% effort with 5 seconds rest intervals.
4. 1,000 metres backstroke with hand paddles.
5. 5 × 200 metres I.M. departing every 3 minutes.

6. 1,500 metres effort at 90% aiming for absolute steady 100 metres splits throughout, e.g. 1:10, 1:12, 1:12, 1:12, etc.
Afternoon total—7,000 metres

Middle Distance Swimmers' Afternoon Programme, Tuesday

4,500 metres freestyle in one hour, concentrate on technique for the early sections then build up your speed, finishing near 90% effort for the last 1,500 metres.

Middle Distance Swimmers' Afternoon Programme, Thursday

3 × 1,500 metres freestyle efforts departing every 20 minutes. The times to be 18 minutes, 18 mins. 30 secs., 17 mins. 50 secs.
Afternoon totals—9,000 metres

Poolside Exercises

Do this exercise at the completion of each session. Work in pairs. Swimmer one stands on his hands and is kept steady in that position by swimmer two who grasps his ankles. Each swimmer to walk on his hands slowly and firmly for 200 yards/metres. This will take at least a week to master. Exercise number two next week.

Stage Two ....

Sprinters
Weekly total—57,250 yards
Allotted grand total—57,250 yards
Allotted grand total—57,250 yards
Your personal grand total—................

Middle Distance
Weekly total—81,000 yards
Allotted grand total—81,000 yards
Your personal grand total—................

Work Sheet No. 12. Confidential

December 1, 1975

Dear Swimmers,
You impressed me with your performances at the Hall of Fame swim meet. I have enclosed a press cutting. This is the end of our third month together and it is appropriate that we record some of your improvements. You still have a long way to go. But the goals are attainable. We will repeat last week's schedule because, as you

know, no one reached the target due to a slight ease back for the meet. However, I have included Exercise No. 2, so now you do Exercises 1 and 2 at the end of each session at poolside.

Experimental Squad Improvements

Alan Webster, 400 metres I.M., 5:10·6 down to 4:59·2
Bill Young, 1,500 metres freestyle, 17:48·1 down to 17:03·6
Chuck Grace, 200 metres freestyle, 2:14·4 down to 2:11·3
Ken Fitzpatrick, 100 metres breaststroke, 1:19·8 down to 1:17·4
Paula Parris, 800 metres freestyle, 9:41·9 down to 9:14·8
Kathy Becker, 400 metres I.M., 5:36·1 down to 5:26·6

Poolside Exercise No. 2

Floating vertically at the deep end place your hands on the deck, palms down at shoulder width. Pull up and then press until your arms are straight and your body well out of the water. Return to the in-water position. Do this exercise rhythmically thirty times by watching the clock and working at the rate of one push-up each five seconds. Since the deck is one foot above water level I do not want you to kick your legs or undulate to start the movement. Use your arms only.

Work Sheet No. Confidential

December 8, 1975

Dear Swimmers,

Obviously our system is achieving good results, as proved by the fine swims at Miami. Paula, your 100 yards freestyle swim was a fine effort. You are the first of our select squad to make Olympic qualifying trial times. Alan, you are now less than two seconds away from the national age records for the 400 metres freestyle and the 400 metres I.M. We will make a concentrated effort to shatter these times before your fifteenth birthday. Ken, excuse the misprint in the newspaper cutting, your 100 yards butterfly time was 1:01·7. Your best swim however, was the 400 metres I.M. in 5:24·9.

Sprinters' Morning Programme, Monday through Saturday

1. 500 yards I.M. as a loosen-up.
2. 20 × 50 yards freestyle sprints departing every 60 seconds and aiming for 28 seconds each sprint.
3. 500 yards backstroke with hand paddles and legs tied at a good speed.
4. 20 × 50 yards freestyle sprints departing every 1 min. 15 secs. and aiming for 27 seconds each sprint.
5. 500 yards breaststroke with hand paddles.

6. 20 × 50 yards freestyle sprints with the legs tied departing every 60 seconds and aiming for minus 33 seconds.
7. 10 × 100 yards kicking with board departing every 1 min. 50 secs. and working really hard until your legs ache.
Morning total—5,500 yards

Sprinters' Afternoon Programme, Monday, Wednesday and Friday

1. 250 metres butterfly followed by 250 metres breaststroke as a loosen-up.
2. 10 × 100 metres main stroke sprints departing every 2 mins. 30 secs. and swimming within 5 seconds of your best time on every sprint.
3. 20 × 25 metres freestyle kick sprints departing every 40 seconds.
4. 10 × 75 metres sprints departing every 2 minutes and aiming for minus 46 seconds for freestylers.
5. 10 × 25 metres dolphin kick sprints departing every 40 seconds.
6. 10 × 50 metres freestyle sprints departing every 1 min. 15 secs., all sprints to be under 29 seconds from push.
7. 500 metres relaxing backstroke.
8. 20 × 25 metres main stroke sprints at absolute maximum speed, departing every 45 seconds.
9. 500 metres dead slow freestyle, relaxing and thinking!
Afternoon total—5,000 metres

Sprinters' Afternoon Programme, Tuesday and Thursday

1. 500 metres I.M. as a loosen up.
2. 10 × 100 I.M. departing every 2 mins. 30 secs., all to be under 1 min. 10 secs.
3. 500 metres dolphin kick, doing as much of this as possible underwater.
4. 1,500 metres of your main stroke with alternate 100 metres of very fast and very slow throughout.
Afternoon total—3,500 metres

Middle Distance Swimmers' Morning Programme, Monday through Saturday

1. 5 × 400 yards I.M. with 15 seconds rest between each effort. All to be within 20 seconds of your best time.
2. 1,000 yards fast kicking with flippers and board.
3. 3 × 800 metres efforts at 85%, 95%, 90%.
4. 15 × 100 yards sprints departing every 1 min. 40 secs. and working very hard. Use hand paddles and leg ties throughout.
5. 40 × 25 metres sprints departing every 30 seconds, various strokes.
Morning total—7,900 yards

Middle Distance Swimmers' Afternoon Programme, Monday, Wednesday and Friday

1. 250 metres left arm, 250 metres right arm on freestyle or backstroke.
2. 20 × 200 metres freestyle efforts departing every 2 mins. 45 secs. and aiming for negative splits, each effort to be held absolutely steady on 2 mins. 20 secs.
3. 500 metres relaxed freestyle kicking.
4. 30 × 50 metres legs tied sprints departing every 45 seconds.
5. 20 × 25 metres butterfly sprints breathing every 3 strokes and departing every 30 seconds.

Afternoon total—7,000 metres

Middle Distance Swimmers' Afternoon Programme, Tuesday and Thursday

1. 1,500 metres freestyle in about 18 minutes. Have just enough rest to put on your hand paddles and do
2. 1,500 metres freestyle with hand paddles in less than 20 minutes. Have just enough rest to take off your paddles and put on your leg tie band, then do
3. 1,500 metres freestyle with legs tied.

Afternoon total—4,500 metres ....

Sprinters
Weekly total—57,200 yards
Allotted grand total—114,450 yards
Your personal grand total—................

Middle Distance
Weekly total—80,400 yards
Allotted grand total—161,400 yards
Your personal grand total—................

7. The freestyle sprint today

Le Style, c'est l'homme.

The stroke techniques used by today's sprint champions should be adequate to create new records for at least a decade—it will be some time yet before the 100 metres records bottom. Greater body size and superior strength, more specific training, facilities amenable to speed swimming and that magic ingredient, the passing of time, will be the main reasons for the progression.

Because of the body's limitation to speed through water it is doubtful if the present day freestyle technique, which has been virtually unchanged for 50 years, can be altered greatly. Coaches and swimmers however, should cultivate enquiring minds and question the validity of today's styles.

As the sprinter's speed approaches eight feet a second we will have to give greater attention to principles we have taken for granted, being mindful that minor technical errors and areas of resistance are magnified by the theoretical square law. Theoreticians South African Cecil Colwin and Canadian Howard Firby, are stroke perfectionists who are constantly seeking advances in style. There are many other thoughtful coaches and physiologists who are looking for a stroke breakthrough. Some top coaches believe this breakthrough will come when we learn to undulate the body similarly to the movements of the dolphin and superimpose this over the present freestyle arm and kicking actions.

When one observes the fluid action and apparent ease of propulsion by aquatic mammals that undulate, it does seem a possibility that man, by crudely imitating, can improve his water prowess in a limited way. I have often observed the seals and dolphins in Australian and Hawaiian centres and have been amazed at their vertical leaps of nearly 20 feet with only a few tail flicks and a couple of body waves. Their smooth skin surfaces and contours, their streamlined noses and heads, their flexibility and power-packed tails, places them, pound for pound, well ahead of us in water power.

Some things we should examine are the possibilities of developing a smoother contour for our sprinters, a substance or a means to lower the water resistance on the body surface area, the extension of the role of the legs and the feet in propulsion (the leg muscles are the most powerful in the body), the use of drills to strengthen parts of the stroke in the water. Items such as Howard Firby's chicken wings, fist swimming or the author's pectoral pulls, will all open up avenues of investigation in the development of the stroke and its more efficient execution.

The left hand reaches a point underneath the chest as the right hand makes the entry

1

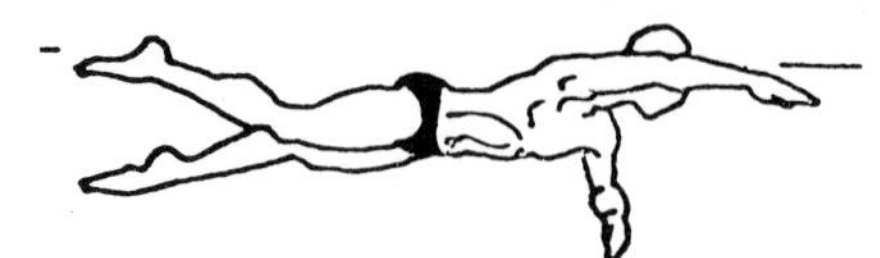

The left hand reaches maximum pushing power as the right hand takes up the pulling position

2

The right hand is starting to pull as the left arm commences recovery

3

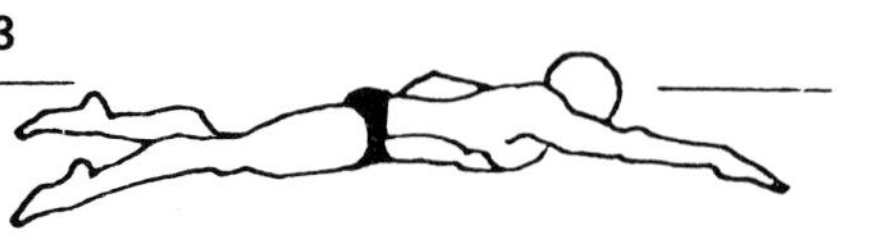

The two arms are now starting to work opposite each other. The pull is gaining power, the recovering arm lifting

4

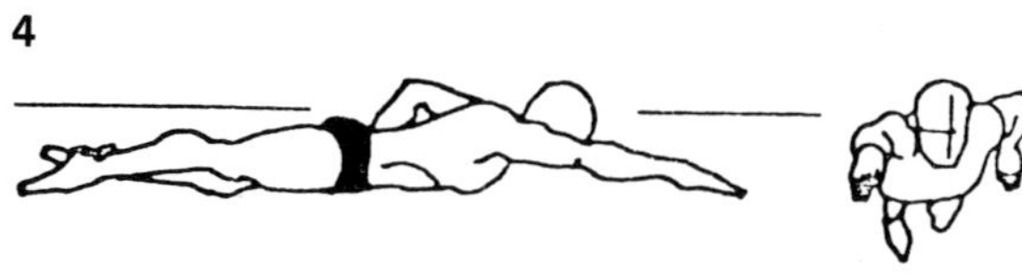

The sprinter's arm is recovered quickly as the pulling arm begins its boomerang bend

5

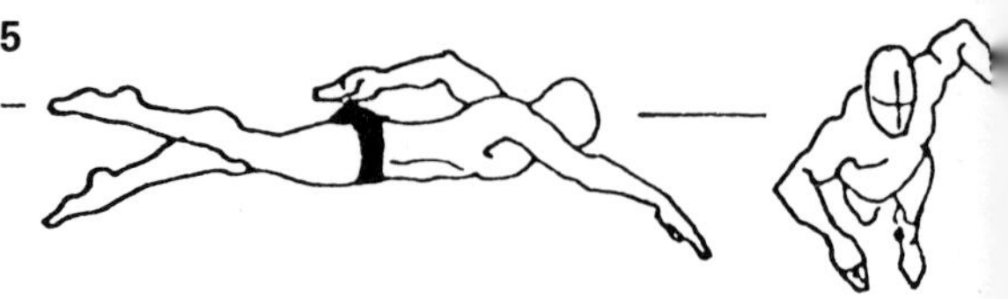

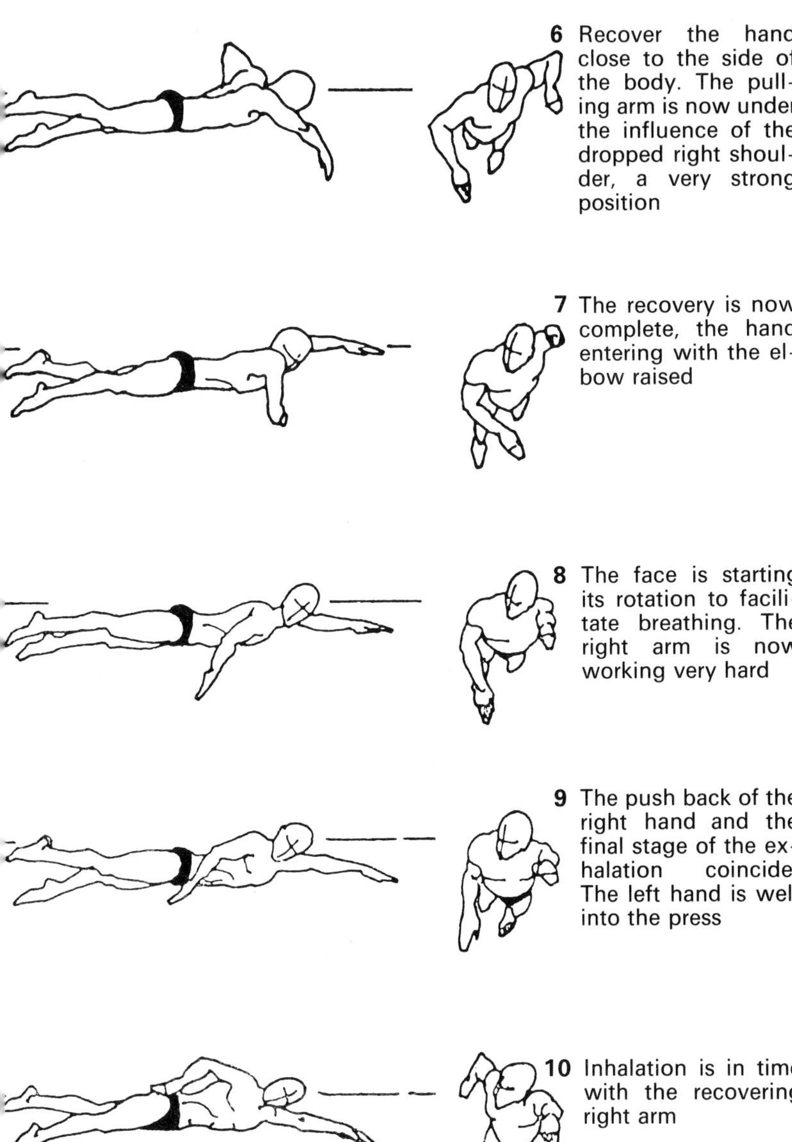

6 Recover the hand close to the side of the body. The pulling arm is now under the influence of the dropped right shoulder, a very strong position

7 The recovery is now complete, the hand entering with the elbow raised

8 The face is starting its rotation to facilitate breathing. The right arm is now working very hard

9 The push back of the right hand and the final stage of the exhalation coincide. The left hand is well into the press

10 Inhalation is in time with the recovering right arm

The Body

Fish are completely submerged and the incompressibility of the water determines to some degree the shape of their body, which nature makes ideal for their needs. Moving underwater they experience less resistance than swimming on the surface. The human body floats with up to 95 per cent of its bulk submerged and when pulled through the water in this position it creates double resistance by producing waves in front of the head, eddies in the small of the back, drag over the buttocks plus the resistance of the huge bulk of the chest, shoulders, arms, stomach and legs. Because of this double resistance, man's efficiency in water is very poor. The body in motion must lie flat and in as resistance-free position as possible, not only in the lateral plane (protruding elbows and forearms, or side whipping the lower legs) but also in the horizontal alignment (dropped stomach, dropped elbows, too deep a flutter kick or excessive knee bend).

I teach a body position where the shoulders are high, allowing the water to slide under the smooth contours of the chest and stomach. The bend in the frame should be just enough to avoid placing the thighs, knees and lower legs excessively deep. The head should tilt slightly forward, resembling somewhat the alignment of the Concorde aircraft with its nose section bent down. This head tilt counterbalances the depth of the leg drive.

One must aim to position high without using excessive muscular stress to do so. The object is to use nearly all the available energy to propel oneself forward. It is an advantage therefore, to have a body whose floatation is good enough to hold a fair proportion of the frame out of the water. The larger-boned or heavier-boned sprinter will have as much as thirty per cent more resistance than the high floater with a light or thin skeleton. Excessive muscle bulk also plays a detrimental part in trying to float high.

The sprinter with heavy bones and over-bulked muscles is at a distinct disadvantage since muscle and bone do not float. This disadvantage is magnified greatly as the distance swum is increased. The observant coach will realise that there is an optimum body position for each individual sprinter and that holding the body position too high may be too costly in terms of energy expended to counteract anti-gravitational pull. Normal high floaters who have occasionally competed in salt water pools remark of being too high out of the water, because of the greater buoyancy, and of 'losing grip', whereas heavy-boned sprinters position correctly in salt water and usually swim improved times. This is also one reason why some average pool swimmers often become above-average surf swimmers. The tenseness of the muscles decrees floatability, a tense body has much more difficulty in floating and especially staying on an even keel. Relaxation with muscle tone is desirable.

The speed and the angle with which the arms are recovered also influences the body position and floatation. The recovery must be fast so that the weight of the arm (in excess of 10 pounds) does not push the body lower into the water. The recovery of the forearms must be close to the side of the body so that the lateral sway of the hips does not occur by executing a wide or low recovery. The head position for sprinters can be unnecessarily high. Fraser and Schollander, almost perfect strokers, carried their heads a fraction too high.

A simple but dramatic demonstration as to the role of the head and its influence on the body's position in the water can be shown by having the sprinter float with his face well down in the water. This he will achieve easily. Then have the swimmer try to float with his face held up high out of the water—he will sink. Sprinting with the head too high is not the most advantageous position for speed.

The Breathing

Bi-lateral breathing is of little use to sprinters, except perhaps to observe other swimmers in training or competition. Bi-lateral limits the sprinter's performance. It controls the swimmer instead of the opposite being the desirable situation. Shane Gould, a noted bi-lateral breather, held the world 100 metres freestyle record, but in her swims over this distance she used bi-lateral only for short bursts. The breathing action leaves very little area with which to experiment. There are only a few anatomical movements possible.

Work is needed now to check the best breathing pattern for individual sprinters to use. Turning the head does fractionally slow down the speed. Those least efficient in the smooth action of turning the head to breathe lose most speed. The obvious thing is to cover a sprint distance with the least number of breaths. However, since this will escalate a premature build-up of the oxygen debt, an agreeable ratio has to be found between the distance covered and the minimum number of breaths. Here are the breathing patterns of some adult champions over 100 metres:

25 metres pool	**50 metres pool**
25 metres 2 to 4 times	
50 metres 5 to 8 times	50 metres 10 to 21 times
75 metres 8 to 10 times	
100 metres 6 to 10 times	100 metres 26 to 36 times

I advocate taking a breath on each arm cycle in training. The inhalation through the mouth should be adequate but not too deep or full. Films taken underwater often show bubbles emitting from the nostrils during the exhalation phase; some of this air is air trapped in the nostrils, naturally. The balance of air is air squeezed out as a consequence of pressure building up in the nasal passages. You should not try to exhale through the nose.

Breathing too deeply will "tie up" the sprinter, may cause coughing or even dizziness, certainly make him feel very tight across the chest. The inhalation takes place at water level or slightly below water level, just behind the bow wave created by the head. A side-on view at water level of a speeding sprinter will prove that the breath is actually taken in, below water level. Once the breath is taken it is held slightly and exhalation actually commences when the face is pointing directly down to the bottom of the pool. A firm and regular stream of spent air is exhaled as the face returns to the side position, with the final puff coming just as the mouth clears the water. This final puff also clears water from around the mouth area and facilitates the inhalation.

The shoulders should rotate smoothly and this rhythmical roll facilitates breathing by placing the mouth advantageously for the intake. Most mentors teach the breathing pattern by having the pupil rotate his head independently on the neck axis so that the shoulders do not roll excessively. But in actual advanced technique the head is 'locked in' to a comfortable mould on the shoulders. There is very little independent movement of the head.

Jon Konrads, ex-multiple world record holder in freestyle, had an exemplary breathing technique. The method he used is now followed by millions. The head was held at the hairline, not too high or too low. The rhythm between his arm turnover and the movement of his head was ideal. His head appeared to be firmly attached to his shoulder girdle and yet he did not roll his shoulders unduly in order to place his face in a good breathing position.

A beautiful rollicking rhythm can be perfected by swimmers who learn to minimise their head movements and extend their mouths sideways in the inhalation phase. Nothing looks more disjointed than the swimmer who makes two inter-dependent head movements to turn his face out of the water or to return his face into the water. This lack of coordination is often reflected in other parts of the stroke e.g. the arm recovery, the kick.

Some stroke technicians advocate not turning the face to breathe until the fingers of the hand on the non-breathing side of the body are actually well down (3 or 4 inches) into the water. This was the method taught to Dawn Fraser in her stroke-forming days. Nowadays, especially with high turnover stroke-makers, it is better to start to turn the head to breathe just as the fingers reach the water. The timing of the head back to centre is usually signalled by the recovering arm on the breathing side. Today's sprinters start to move the face back to centre a fraction of time after the recovering hand has passed the face. The hand reaches the water fractionally before the face centres. Some sprint coaches like the thumb and the nose to align on the centre line simultaneously.

The Catch and Press Stage

The importance of the hands in the catch position is emphasised if one tries fist swimming. In fist swimming there is a tendency for the body to lose balance, the arms to dive down too quickly, the entry to be rough. The hand entry plays an important role in regulating to some extent, the maximum speed at which the arm can be forced through the water. The larger the 'paddle' the slower the pull and push cycle. Common errors in hand placement are the submerging of the wrist before the fingers, thus allowing a loss of grip or pressure. The taking down of a stream of bubbles on the fingertips or the protruding thumbs indicates a loss of efficiency and an unclean entry. This is to be avoided. Even advanced sprinters often do not appreciate the importance of experimenting with the angle of the flat of the hand in the press against the water. Obviously, the fingers should be held together but no great pressure should be applied in the abduction movement to hold a firm hand. Underwater photographs show that some sprinters do have a slight split between fingers, but it is only minor.

Some sprinters catch, pull and push with the thumb slightly leading. This is wrong because it places the hands at an angle where the pressure is allowed to slip off the little finger side of the hand. The hand should be held flat upon entry with the fingers straight, with the thumb lying neatly alongside the forefinger. There should be firmness in the wrist and firmness through the fingers. The wrist should be raised into a cocked position. Land training programmes should include strengthening exercises for the wrists and fingers. These exercises also flow on to the lower forearm which gains in strength. This area is often neglected in strengthening systems.

The hand enters the water with the thumb directly in front of, or just a fraction outside of, the line of the nose. Pressure is initiated at the fingertips and this often elusive feel of the water must be held through the three phases of the underwater movement, that is, the press, the pull and the push. Superior sprinting champions report that they do feel pressure on their fingertips, whereas novice swimmers do not. The principles of hand entry taught to me many years ago still applies—the fingertips make a clean hole in the water for the wrist to push into, the wrist makes the hole larger for the elbow to enter. This emphasises the fact that the elbow should never reach or enter the water before the hand. Coaches ensure this by insisting upon a high elbow recovery.

The hand and arm should find maximum press as soon as possible, then commence their downward movement, which is with the hand along the centre line. Do not bend the elbow too soon as this may allow the elbow to drop, causing slip and the loss of power. When the hand has reached a position where the arm forms an angle of forty-five degrees to the surface, the arm starts to bend so that the elbow points outwards and the hand starts to move across the centre line. The amount of bend at the elbow is individual to every sprinter but the angle should never be greater than ninety degrees. Laboratory testing has proved that the arm's strongest pulling and pushing position is when the elbow is bent ninety degrees. The weakest position is when the arm is held straight. As the hand is at that forty-five degrees mark as mentioned previously, the elbow bends very quickly and very noticeably so that it is just outside the line of the body and the hand is right along the centre line. When the hand reaches a point underneath the navel it pushes across to the opposite hip. Care should be taken that the hand does not go outside the body line as this will cause the shoulder of the pushing arm to drop and the body's balance is impaired. The hand then describes an arc to a point some four inches below the bottom of the swimsuit from where it will start to recover. Keep the hand flat to retain pressure almost to the end of the stroke. At the last moment the hand will turn so that the little finger leads out of the water.

The pull and push diagrammatically resembles an elongated, inverted question mark. The last part of the push should be four to six inches down in the water. A shallow finish is a loss of power. The rolling of the shoulder will aid the forearm and hand in maintaining a forceful finish to the push. There is gradual acceleration throughout the stroke, care being taken not to pull the hand through the water so rapidly that it cuts holes in the water. The press section should be firm and fast, the pull section faster and the final push section the fastest part of the stroke. The underwater timing between the two hands is:— when the leading hand is six inches below the surface the finishing hand is six inches from the end of the stroke. This timing guarantees maximum pressure being applied continuously. It also regulates the turnover rate.

The Recovery

The recovery must be neat. There is no international swimmer who has an untidy recovery. Some coaches have been known to say that it doesn't really matter much what happens on top of the water, it's what you do underneath that counts. This is true if you wish to remain merely a club swimmer without much pride in your water appearance. Perfectionists in recovery have been almost machine-like. Their timing, their high elbow lift, their clean hand placement has given them style that is remembered, copied and spoken about. It is a reasonable assumption that, if one takes pride in the above water phase, adequate thought will be given to the working segment of the stroke below.

Those fortunate enough to have seen Murray Rose, Jon Konrads, Dawn Fraser, and Don Schollander in the 1960s, or Rick DeMont, Mark Spitz and Jim Montgomery in the 1970s, will know what I mean when I write about a clean recovery. Not many swimmers realise that the recovery deteriorates as the swimmer gets older, or should I say as he physically matures.

The neatest stylists are the lithe-body types who manage to spear into the water without undue disturbance of the surface. As the body bulks across the shoulders and the upper arms (with maturity) it becomes increasingly difficult to have a clean or high recovery. Many times I have seen all-time great sprinters recovering high and precisely when their bodies have been covered with just the right amount of muscle. Two classic examples I can recall were super sprinters Shane Gould and Dawn Fraser. The older and heavier they became the less precise and the lower their recoveries became.

The working shoulder, that is the one in the water, must be used to assist the recovering arm. By rolling the working shoulder down (to reinforce the strength of the underwater push) the lift of the recovering arm is facilitated. Do not roll the shoulder too deep, this will cause the body to go off balance, but work the shoulders in unison, as the working shoulder drops the recovering elbow lifts. The elbow must be the first part of the arm to leave the water, the fingers the last, in the recovery.

In heavy training the recovery often drops low or wide but the mechanics of a good recovery improve as the swimmer is allowed to freshen up, usually during the taper-down period. Mark Spitz was particularly fortunate in that his lithe body allowed him to execute clean and precise recovery movements. Mike Wenden was the other end of the scale and his low, sweeping recovery never looked classical. Spitz never had to work much on his recovery whereas Wenden's stroke was often so low that the fingers and elbows touched the water midway through the recovery.

What then constitutes the ideal recovery? First of all, the recovering arm must be brought forward in such a manner that it does not influence the horizontal plane. A low, wide, sweeping arm affects the opposite hip causing lateral sway. An arm that recovers with the hand higher than the elbow wastes time (the hand has to describe a semi-circle) and often allows the elbow to enter the water before the hand. Therefore, at the end of the stroke, lead the hand out of the water little finger first, lift the elbow high and rotate the shoulder forward. Make sure that at all times the fingers are close to the water line and that the hand is always lower than the elbow.

Keep the hand close to the side of the body as it is moved forward. The hand is normally relaxed and the fingers trail behind. When the elbow has reached the halfway point in the recovery swing the lower arm towards the centre line in front of the head. Let the shoulder roll forward but do not let it over-extend. An over-extended shoulder and a stretched straight arm nearly always enters the water in the weakest position for the catch. The elbow and the wrist should be slightly cocked as the hand reaches the water for this now is the end of the relaxed section of the recovery and firmness must take over for the press.

Front-on observation nearly always shows that the arms recover differently. Usually the breathing-side arm recovers the higher and the wider of the two. A simple drill to "educate" the arms into similar recoveries is to have the sprinter swim down the pool as close to the side wall as practicable. This will ensure a high elbow lift and the constant knocking of his hand against the side wall will soon cause him to keep the hand very close to the side of the body during recovery. Have the sprinter return up the pool so that the other arm is disciplined. From a side-on view the coach can detect if elbows are lifting equally and if the hands are equi distance from the surface.

The Underwater Arm Sequence

Throughout this century, the underwater positioning of the two arms has changed often only to return to a system used earlier. In the 1920s, Kojac, Kealoha and Weissmuller used a timing where one hand was more than halfway through the stroke as the recovering hand entered the water. These swimmers had strong six beat kicks.

In the late 1940s, the Japanese evolved a long, stretched-out gliding style in which one hand was at the beginning of the pull section as the other hand entered the water. These swimmers created numerous world freestyle records. Their six beat kick was extremely well developed and when one looks back in retrospect it appears that their successes were due to superior conditioning more so than technique.

Lorraine Crapp, the first woman to better five minutes for 400 metres, was a close adherent to this style. This was during the mid 1950s. At this point Australia produced the greatest group of sprinters in its history. Their respective arm timings were:

Jon Henricks, hand entering, other hand five-eights of the way through the stroke;

John Devitt, hand entering, other hand seven-eights of the way through the stroke;

Gary Chapman, hand entering, other hand three-quarters of the way through the stroke;

Dawn Fraser, hand entering, other hand half-way through the stroke;

Lorraine Crapp, hand entering, other hand quarter-way through the stroke;

Faith Leech, hand entering, other hand half-way through the stroke.

Fraser, Crapp and Henricks were superb kick exponents, whereas Devitt had to persevere to move the kick board. These sprinters between them, took all the freestyle sprint medals in the 1956 Olympics. Devitt and Fraser, retaining their 1956 techniques, won the Olympic sprint titles in 1960. Dawn Fraser completed the hat trick by winning the sprint title for the third time in 1964 with a style unchanged for eight years.

Sprinters who use kicks other than the recognised six beat usually have one hand entering the water and the other hand three-quarters of the way through the push. Olympic champion Mike Wenden, was of this school.

Mark Spitz has the classic style, one hand entering the water as the other hand reaches the umbilicus. Therefore, the recommended timing is:

* For strong six beat kickers, one hand entering the water as the

other hand is halfway through the underwater stroke;

* for swimmers with a weak leg trail, kicking action, one hand entering the water as the other hand reaches a point seven-eights through the underwater stroke;
* for swimmers with a four beat kick cross-over, one hand entering the water as the other hand reaches a point three-quarters through the underwater stroke;
* for swimmers with a two beat crossover kicking action, one hand entering the water as the other hand reaches a point three-quarters through the underwater stroke.

The Extent of Bending the Arm Underwater

If we had unlimited strength it would be logical to pull and push the arms in a straight position for the entire underwater action. Man makes best movement on land and through water by the use of bending movements. Athletic coaches insist on high knee lifting in running. Swimming coaches recommend bending the arms underwater in order to distribute the available energy provided by all the muscles of the arm equally.

Very early this century the flailing over-arm action was accompanied by a fairly straight pull. This pull was usually outside the line of the body. During the 1920s a bend in the elbow was introduced but the hand did not traverse down the centre line. It was not until the 1940s that the coaches started to experiment with a bent arm pull and push as a means towards greater speed through the water. Classically it was thought that the ideal would be to have the hands catch, pull and push directly along the centre line with a quick "sweep-out" at the end of the stroke. Soon it was realised that in order to obtain the optimum power from the shoulder and chest muscles the hand would have to move across the centre line. The second reasoning behind this was that the bend should push into undisturbed water from whence maximum force could be obtained.

Devitt of Australia developed a style where the hand started along the centre line and pushed right across the opposite hip. Often the hand went so far across that it passed outside the line of the body. This was certainly a vigorous stroke that needed much shoulder power and a fast turnover in order to succeed. This technique was brought to its greatest development in 1968 by Michael Wenden. Wenden refined the style by moving the hands across the centre line but not outside the line of the body.

Today's champions take full advantage of the shoulder power by rolling the shoulder on to the stroke as it starts its pushing action. The hand cuts across the centre line and this is where the elbow is at its maximum bend. In this position the hand and the forearm present a wide, flat surface to the water. Underwater films show that some sprinters have the hand as close as six inches below the chest as it pushes through. This is a little too close, twelve to fifteen inches below the chest is the better position.

The Kicking Action

The greatest sprinters will be those who will have naturally, a "whippy" leg drive. By naturally I mean a kick that does not have to be taught—only refined. These long-legged "whippy" kickers come closest, together with the dolphin kickers, to the piscine mode of movement. Long leg muscles, thin ankles, and longer than average feet are pre-requisites for a good kick.

The kicking action should balance the stroke. It must not be too deep and only on the most vigorous sprints should the feet cause turbulence above the water. The lower the under leg drives down the greater the resistance build-up to the forward movement. It is impossible to keep the legs within a line defined by the thickness of the body. But you should try not to let the lower leg drop too deep below the line of the chest and the stomach. The kick emanates from the hip joint, there is a slight flexing at the knee. Thigh kickers are the fastest, knee kickers do the most work for the least result. It is necessary to turn the feet slightly inwards in order to obtain maximum push against the water in both the upward and downward movement.

Sprinters should take care not to "toe-in" excessively as this causes the knees to spread and too large a gap to appear between the lower legs. The ideal kicking action is one where the feet replace each other in position. As the top leg moves down it describes an arc until it reaches the lowest part of its downward drive. The bottom leg moves upward simultaneously describing its arc and reaching the point from where the top leg started.

The kicking action can be improved greatly with practice. Very little study has been given to conditioning the body as a whole with extensive kicking drills. Shortage of time or disinterest by coaches are the reasons for this. Several coaches have reported marked improvement in conditioning and kicking speed by working the team on super speed kick sprints with flippers. The vigorous use of flippers certainly extends ankle flexbility, tightens the thigh muscles and educates the legs into kicking correctly. (See reference to flipper kicking in Chapter 6.) Adult sprinters have been under the sixty seconds for the 100 metres freestyle kick with the flippers.

The kicks used for freestyle distance and sprinting are the same, only the tempo is different. The present day kick styles are:

1. the narrow, fast, six-beat kick as used by the world's sprint record holders today;
2. the four-beat crossover kick used by some sprinters almost in world class, and many 400 metres freestyle swimmers;

3. the two-beat with legs trail kick used by distance swimmers and a few sprinters.

Essentials in Freestyle Sprint Stroking

1. Body position:
* Move through the water in a high position.
* Minimise resistance by assuring that there are no protruding forearms or elbows, that the kick does not work outside the lateral plane.
* Minimise resistance horizontally by assuring that the kick is not too deep, the knees are not bent too much, or that the elbows are not dropped.
* The body must be firm but not stiff.

2. Breathing:
* Take a breath on each arm cycle in normal training.
* Pivot the head on the central axis to breathe.
* Do not turn the head too far back in order to inhale.
* View sideways or slightly in front when inhaling. Do not look back.
* Distort the mouth sideways in order to facilitate inhalation.
* Turn the head to breathe just as the non-breathing side fingers tip the water.
* Return the head to centre just after the breathing side hand has passed the face.
* The head should be held so that the water line is almost up to the hairline.

3. Catch, press and push:
* The hand enters the water with the thumb just outside the line of the nose.
* Slightly cock the wrist so that the hand is firm and feels the catch immediately.
* Do not drop the elbow at any point of the underwater work.
* Do not lead with the thumb first in the press, for preference lead slightly with the little finger.
* Tidy up your entry by making sure that there is no excessive splash and that you do not take a stream of bubbles down with the hand.
* Keep the fingers together with the thumb neatly placed alongside the forefinger.
* Do not drop the shoulder too early in the press stage as this will cause a loss of grip and power.
* Pull the hand along the centre line for the first third of the stroke then start moving it across to the opposite hip.
* Make sure that you push the hand at least four inches past the bottom of the bathers before ending the stroke.

* The end of the stroke should be in deep water (from four to six inches) in order to maintain effective pressure.

4. Recovery:

* At the end of the stroke the first part of the arm to emerge from the water is the elbow, not the hand.
* A high bent elbow recovery is the most relaxed way to move the arm forward.
* Point the elbow high and make sure that the hand moves forward just above the surface of the water, close to the side of the body.
* Rotate the shoulder forward to allow for ease of reach.
* Work the underwater shoulder in unison with the recovering shoulder so that the dropping of the underwater shoulder assists the lifting of the recovering arm.
* The hand enters the water with the elbow and wrist cocked.
* The hand enters the water with the thumb slightly leading. This position assures that no bubble stream is taken down on the fingers.
* The hand entry must be between the shoulder line and the nose line.

5. The kicking action:

* Do not drop the hips, this will cause a side whip-kick outside the alignment of forward progression.
* The kick emanates from the hip joint. It must be relatively straight with a slight hinging movement at the knee and ankle on the downward drive.
* Do not bend the knees excessively as this will drop them below the line of forward progression. It will also cause the feet to lift out of the water.
* Cultivate a push from the upward kicking movement of the foot as well as the downward thrust of the foot.
* A six beat kick is preferable, that is, six beats to each complete arm cycle. If you are by nature, not capable of a six beat kick, develop and condition your present kicking action.
* Develop a whipping-foot action with the big toe turned slightly inwards on the downward thrust.
* Keep the legs close to each other.

6. The freestyle start:

* On "take your mark", step to your position, curl your toes over the edge of the starting block and bend forward with your hands dangling down in front of you and your eyes looking into the water some six feet in front.
* The feet are about six inches apart for the adult sprinter.
* When the gun goes off commence moving your arms in an anti-clockwise circular movement.
* When your hands are at a point above your head bend your knees and lift your heels.

* Continue your arms down the back as you start to lift your head.
* The arms move forward past the face and as they do you spring forward with the head held high.
* You plane out over the water and just before the hands are about to enter the water, drop the head down.
* The angle of entry is at about twenty degrees and the body is kept straight for a streamlined glide.

7. The grab start:

* On "take your mark", step to your position, curl your toes over the edge of the starting block, stretch your hands down and curl your fingers under the edge of the starting block or press your fingers back against the front edge of the starting block if the block does not have a lip.
* The feet are about four inches apart and the hands grab just outside the little toes.
* When the gun goes off press back firmly against the block with the hands, drop the shoulders down vigorously and you will start to overbalance.
* As you start to roll forward press firmly with your toes and at the same time, start to lift your head.
* Push out hard and stretch out over the water in a straight position.
* Drop the head as the hands reach the water and streamline into the pool with a minimum of resistance.

8. The Tennessee variation:

* Recently it has been found that by entering the water with the body slightly piked the underwater distance covered is increased if the body straightens when half the torso is submerged. This causes a large body wave or undulating movement.
* The trajectory through the air should be slightly higher than normal.
* The body enters the water slightly short of a normal position.
* It is the sudden straightening of the body and the legs as they enter the water that causes the giant surge forward.
* This start is particularly beneficial for butterfly swimmers.
* This type of start can be emphasised by having young swimmers try to get the feel of it by using flippers when diving from the block.

9. The freestyle tumble turn:

* No other turn but the tumble turn should be taught even with beginners.
* As you approach the wall do not slacken speed.
* View the wall by looking underwater, do not lift your head up.
* When the head is some three feet from the wall drop the head and shoulders forward as if you are going to roll over on a mat.
* Do not roll deeply, try to keep close to the surface.
* When the backs of your shoulders are facing the wall drop one

shoulder lower than the other.

* At this point the hands are tucked neatly by the side of the face.
* The dropping of one shoulder causes the body to do a half twist.
* If we have dropped the left shoulder the legs recover around the left side of the body, with knees bent so that the feet drop onto the wall with the toes extended. Your body is now in a side-on position to the wall because your feet have landed on the wall side-on.
* As you push off vigorously from the wall you should kick to the surface taking your first arm stroke just as your head is about to break the water.
* If you prefer to drop the right shoulder after you have done your half turn your legs are recovered around the right hand side.
* The legs should never be carried straight over but describe a semi-circle at an angle of forty-five degrees to the water.

8. Stephen Holland as an Age Group Swimmer

In view of his undoubted potential, it will be pertinent to consider Stephen Holland, world record holder for the 1500 m. freestyle. Steve was a member of my squad the year before I left Australia. I coached him during part of his very important formative years. I write this section because his training sessions could become milestones of conditioning in Australia, and could be followed to advantage by aspiring distance champions. And as Forbes Carlile said, it was during this time that he made most improvement.

Training characteristics

Steve was unique in his ability to repeat pre-set times in both training and competition. I had little to do with this, except round it off. It was instinctive, but in part it was due to his stroke rate, which varied very little. He would start the training session fresh, stroking at sixty-three strokes for each fifty metres, and he would finish the workout, eight thousand metres later, still working at the same rate. He developed this fast turn-over because of his desire to stay up in training with the older swimmers, Brad Cooper and Graham White, both Olympic distance medallists and members of the team at that time. Steve would go out fast and hang on as long as he could. It was not long before he was up with and then ahead of these champions in training, and later in competitions. He has never altered his fast turn-over.

Stephen's rapid improvement over the longer distances developed because he could handle long and hard loads of "pulling" and "paddles". Being isolated from the mainstreams of hard training, as we were in Australia, I did not realise that Steve was doing more "above-the-waist" work than any other swimmer. His training lists often included as much as five thousand metres of "pull" or "paddles" in one session; he frequently went as high as seventy-five per cent loading on arm-stress work.

He has long tapering legs that float very close to the surface when they are tied, thereby causing a minimum of drag. When he swims without his legs tied he has a "fault" in as much that he drives one leg very deep to balance his stroke. He uses his strong upper-waist power to pull, without undue stress on his shoulders.

In January 1973, Steve developed tendonitis. All serious distance swimmers seem to; Australia's Jenny Turrall, world record holder for 800 m. freestyle, has been troubled with "swimmer's shoulder" for months at a time. Fortunately Steve's resilience is so great that a few days out of the water and a week or two without the legs tied and he bounces right back to good health.

He did not do land exercises, but being an avid surf swimmer (and champion) he obtained, in an enjoyable manner each week-end, heavy loads of running on sand and pulling the life-belt through the heavy seas off the Queensland coast. The double-arm paddling action used to propel a surf board is an ideal way to build strength into the shoulders, back and arms. Surfing can be an advantage to a still-water swimmer if used intelligently. It exercises the whole body vigorously, its fun, and it keeps the swimmer in the water.

Training differences

In planning Steve's programmes I placed "pulling" ahead of "paddles" in priority. We used simple bands of rubber, cut from car inner-tubes, to tie the legs. After a few months I realised that this overload was not sufficient for Steve. He simply breezed along with his legs tied. I made up a series of weighted bands that had a piece of flat lead curled around them. The weight of the lead was two ounces, three ounces and four ounces. We introduced these into the sessions and they became standard equipment. Steve used them every day. The weighted bands do not have effect in the first few lengths of training but their drag becomes accumulative, and it becomes hard going at the end of a session. Steve was the only swimmer who used the "sights" consistently.

Steve disliked kicking on the board. We substituted these sections of the workout with more "pulling". Mike Burton, the winner of two Olympic 500 m. freestyle gold medals, was the last great distance man to work the kick-board seriously. Thirteen per cent of his daily training was on leg-drive conditioning. Tim Shaw, world record holder for the four hundred metres freestyle, uses the kick-board sparingly.

Early years

Holland's early coaching was carried out by his father, the pool manager at Carina, a Brisbane suburb. Steve is the second youngest of five children, and for safety reasons he was taught to swim when he was very young. At three years of age he could splash his way across the municipal pool and he won his first ribbon at five years. He has been in the water practically every day of his life since then, but the early days with his brothers and sisters were fun days.

Australia's great distance champion, Shane Gould, also learnt to swim at the age of three years, in Fiji, and Mark Spitz became a three-year-old water baby when living in Hawaii.

Serious competitive racing started when Steve was twelve years old. His early successes were on the backstroke. He lacked speed on the shorter distances of the front crawl races, and invariably was beaten out of a place. It was not until the events started to lengthen out that he showed some signs of his potential in endurance. At thirteen years he was a skinny kid, almost gaunt, 5 ft. 10 in. high and 112 lb. heavy. He posted some reasonable training times (4:34·6, 9:25·3 and 17:23·0).

The first indication of his imminent greatness came on December 10, 1972, when he easily defeated team-mate and Olympic champion Brad Cooper over 1500 m. freestyle in the Queensland Championships. His time, 16 mins. 35·4 secs., was the fastest in the world that year for a fourteen-year-old boy. To this point he had not broken 17 minutes in

Brad Cooper, Australia's 1972 Olympic 400 m. champion and the first non-American to better 4 min. for the 400 m. freestyle, also reached the Olympic backstroke final. Here he discusses plans with Harry Gallagher; *below, left,* Andy Coan (U.S.A.), fastest man afloat over the short distances, demonstrates the "grab" start. He has returned 51·11 sec. for 100 m. freestyle, this start. Here he is on lane 3; *right,* Steve Holland has an extremely high floatation, his lithe body and light frame being propelled by large hands and feet. A relatively poor sprinter, he is computer-like in his ability to repeat set times

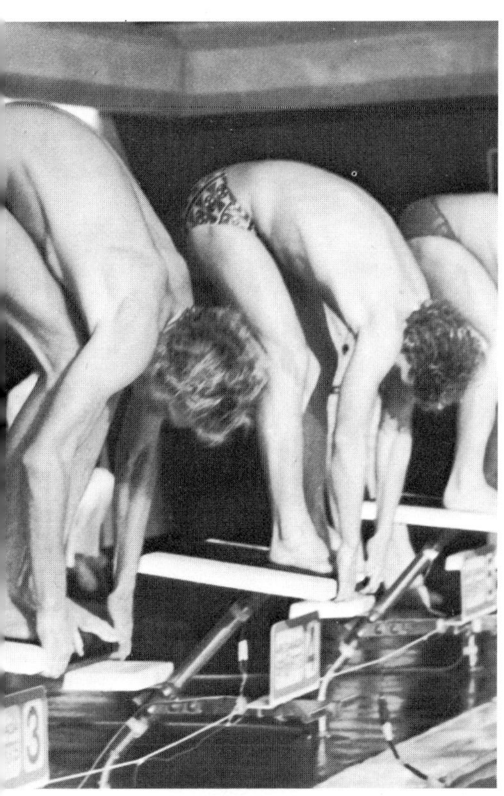

Gallagher corrects Steve Holland's "grab start". The hand positions now accepted are: (a) hands outside the feet; (b) hands between the feet; (c) hands at the side of the block. Holland's start is not strong but Gallagher believes he has the most efficient turn of any distance swimmer in the world; *below,* Holland stretches out like a greyhound for a timed short sprint on a wintry day in Australia

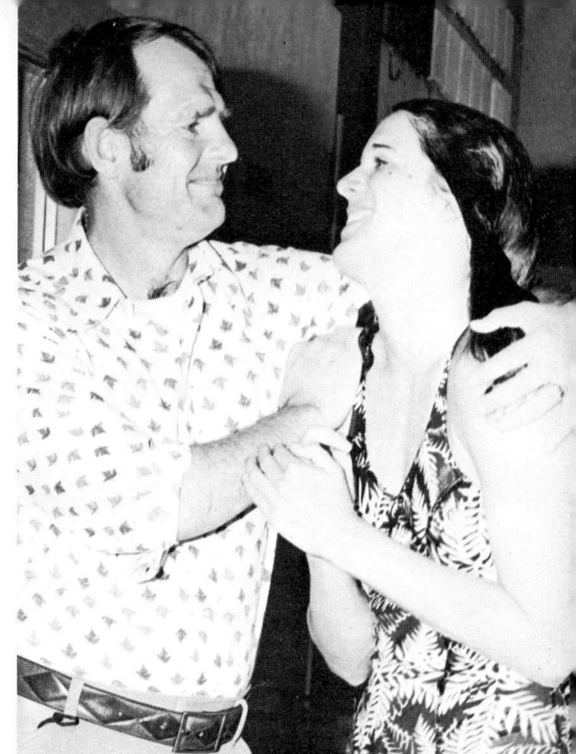

There is a strong bond between most great swimmers and their coaches. Here, Kim Peyton, U.S. sprint star, obviously thinks that her coach Don Jacklin is something special; *below*, Harry Gallagher and Lisa Curry, who at 12 years of age broke the Australian 200 m. individual medley record for her age group

Above, l. to r., Alan Webster, a 13-year-old who improved the Canadian 400 m. individual medley record for his age group; Ken Fitzpatrick, 12, multiple National record holder for the Age Groups in Canada; Kathryn Irvine, 12, whose 9 min. 14 sec. for 800 m. freestyle indicates her potential. All these swimmers used the programme outlined in Chapter 6; *below,* Rick DeMont, U.S.A., right, about to touch out Australia's Brad Cooper at the finish of the Olympic 400 m. in Munich. Cooper was awarded the gold medal on a technicality. Note DeMont's smoother stroke and Cooper's more vigorous arm action caused by doubtful leg drive training (17:04·0) which shows the great motivation he obtains from competition. I mention this because Steve trains very hard, some of his repeat times were really amazing. One is led to think that he could not take much off in a race, but when in tough competition he mesmerizes himself into a painless state of relentless speed. Those who saw the never-to-be-forgotten race against Rick DeMont at Belgrade in 1973 in the World Championships will know what I mean. Steve was so determined to win that he failed to hear the signal indicating "one hundred metres to go". He created a world record for 1500 m. and then continued on at breakneck speed for another hundred metres. Later he said he had no idea of distance, speed or pain during the race.

We continue on the hard distance schedule early in 1973, and by February he had officially reduced his 1500 m. time to 16 mins. 16·6 secs. His 400 m. a sluggish event for him, had improved to 4 mins. 4 secs. These were world-class times, especially at fourteen years of age. Later he recorded 15 min. 58 sec. in training. Steve then transferred to colourful Australian coach Lawrie Lawrence and a few weeks later put up a new world record of 15 mins. 31·5 secs.

Training

Here are two sample training programmes which give the load, the times and the percentages of pulling, paddles and "other strokes", when Steve was a member of my team. His load was steady at five miles each session. Later, with Lawrie Lawrence, it increased to six miles for eleven sessions a week.

Early season, morning: Wt. 120 lb., Ht. 5 ft. 11 in. HR. 47. (water temp. 69 to 71°F.)

1. 10 continuous medleys (2000 m.) in less than 28 minutes.
2. 5 × 400 m. with hand paddles departing every 5 mins. 30 secs. Target time 4 mins. 50 secs.
3. 1000 m. of alternate lengths of butterfly and backstroke.
4. 2 × 1500 m. of freestyle with the legs tied. Each at 90 per cent effort.

Breakdown: Total 8,000 metres in 1 hr. 53 mins.

Paddles	2,000 metres	= 25 per cent
Legs tied	3,000 metres	= $37\frac{1}{2}$ per cent
Other strokes	3,000 metres	= $37\frac{1}{2}$ per cent

Early season, evening

1. 40 × 50 m. of the medley strokes, but in any order, with 10-second rest intervals. Working at 85 per cent effort.
2. 10 × 200 m. freestyle with the legs tied, departing every 2 minutes 45 seconds. Target time 2 minutes 30 seconds.
3. 20 × 100 metres freestyle with hand paddles, departing every 1 minute 15 seconds. Target time 1 minute 9 seconds.
4. 2,000 metres freestyle, starting out at a steady rate and picking up speed throughout. Target time less than 23 minutes and 45 seconds.

Breakdown: Total 8,000 m. in 1 hour 55 minutes.

Paddles	2,000 m.	= 25 per cent
Legs tied	2,000 m.	= 25 per cent
Other Strokes	2,000 m.	= 25 per cent
Main Stroke Effort	2,000 m.	= 25 per cent

Mid season, morning: Wt. 122 lb. Ht. 5 ft. 11 in. HR. 45.

1. 400 m. backstroke, any speed.
2. 600 m. continuous medley, some effort.
3. 10 × 300 m. freestyle with the legs tied, departing every 3 minutes 45 seconds. Target time 3 minutes 30 seconds.
4. 10 × 300 m. freestyle with hand paddles, departing every 3 minutes and 45 seconds. Target time, under 3 minutes and 30 seconds.
5. 1,000 m. of alternate lengths of butterfly and backstroke, with very little emphasis on speed.

Breakdown: Total 8,000 m. in under 2 hours.

Paddles	3,000 m.	= $37\frac{1}{2}$ per cent
Legs Tied	3,000 m.	= $37\frac{1}{2}$ per cent
Other strokes	2,000 m.	= 25 per cent

Mid season, evening:

1. 1,000 m. backstroke with the legs tied, as a stretch out exercise. Easy speed.
2. 10 × 400 m. freestyle efforts, departing every 4 minutes 45 seconds. Target time 4 minutes 30 seconds.
3. 40 × 50 m. "paddle sprints", departing every 45 seconds. Target time 33 seconds or better.
4. 40 × 25 m. "legs tied" sprints, departing every 25 seconds.

Breakdown: Total 8,000 m. in under 2 hours.

Paddles	2,000 m.	= 25 per cent
Legs Tied	1,000 m.	= $12\frac{1}{2}$ per cent
Other strokes	1,000 m.	= $12\frac{1}{2}$ per cent
Main Stroke Effort	4,000 m.	= 50 per cent

Outstanding Training Performances

I have listed her six fine training feats from Stephen Holland as a fourteen-year-old. Other swimmers may, in attempting or bettering these times, set themselves off on the world record road.

January 1973.	4 × 800 m. long course, in 48 minutes. 8:58·8, 8:50·6, 8:57·0, and 8:48·1.
March 1973.	6 × 400 m. long course in 60 minutes. 4:14·1, 4:15·1, 4:13·8, 4:13·6, 4:15·5, 4:16·0.
January 1973.	15 × 100 m. freestyle sprints on the 1 minute 20 seconds.

60·1, 62·2, 62·5, 62·4, 62·6, 62·9, 63·7, 63·2, 63·6, 63·2, 62·9,62·9, 62·6, 62·5, 62·5, 62·0, 61·1.

February 1973. 3 × 1500 m. freestyle in 60 minutes.
17:16·7, 16:58·4 and 16:49·0

February 1973. 5,000 m. non stop.
4·27, 4·39, 4·39, 4·41, 4·38, 4·41, 4·32, 4·35, 4·33, 4·36, 4·38, 4·40, 2·16. = 57 minutes 35 seconds.

March 1973. 4 "broken" 400 m. freestyle swims with 10 seconds rest at the end of each 50 m. Two minutes between each set. Added times: 3:57·7, 3:56·0, 3:56·6, 3:57·0.

9. Crawl sprinting in the U.S.A., by Buck Dawson

Executive Director, International Swimming Hall of Fame

Those of us involved in the pinch of professional sports on amateur swimming are just beginning to be conscious of the greater revenue-producing appeal of short events in the theatre-like environment possible in short course (25 yards and 25 metre) pools. The economics of this situation can hardly be enhanced by the English-speaking world's preoccupation with scuttling yards for metres as soon as possible. Not only is it impossible to convert the thousands of 25 yard pools to 25 metres (and an incredible expense to abandon and build new) but the very concept of a sprint in swimming is lost between the 44 seconds required for the 100 yards Freestyle race and the 51 seconds required for 100 metres Freestyle world time.

Physiologists don't agree on the total number of seconds possible in breath-holding all out effort, but all agree it is less than 45 seconds, that oxygen debt limits are reached in every swimming race longer than 50 metres. To keep exciting all-out swimmers in our sport, we need 50 metre events and we should hold on to our 25 yard short course events.

Amateur Track (athletics) is supported in the United States and Canada by adapting the length of the events to the indoor arenas offering the seating capacity and intimacy that will make it interesting enough to sell tickets. We must make amateur sports promotion financially profitable if it is to flourish in a free enterprise (pro sport) society.

These revenue-producing economic overtones, though often despised by our amateur sports administrators, are a necessary evil if we really want swimming to be taken seriously as a major spectator sport. Even as a strictly participating sport (and swimming in North America certainly has more people involved than any other sport), we must acknowledge that more than half the swimming races in the world are swum in 25 yard short-course pools. Still more would swim (and watch those who swim) if we added the excitement of sprint events to our preoccupation with middle distance swim races (everything over 100 yards), and with aerobic middle distance conditioning. Likewise our scrap pile of early retirees in swimming will be reduced when all swim events do not depend on endurance conditioning. Todays swimming programmes can be likened to a track meet and track training with only the events over 400 metres ($\frac{1}{4}$-mile) allowed on the programme. Why, you say, why indeed as stated by Don Swartz who has trained middle distance star Rick DeMont among others!

> "I don't think we have a true sprint event in swimming with the possible exception of the 50-yard free. My definition of a sprint

> would be an event in which an athlete can go all-out for a given distance."
>
> When John Smith ran one of his great 440s, he split 22·1 and 22·2. I don't know what Lee Evans split when he ran his 43·8, but I am using this track event to correlate it to the 100 free in swimming. There is no evidence that anyone has been able to handle an event at an all-out effort lasting from 40 to 50 seconds in duration. We do have a lot of swimmers who swim all-out in the 100, but they cannot sustain it.
>
> I think that a 25-yard sprint at the nationals would be a hell-of-an-event. If 80,000 people can watch a 100 dash in running lasting 10 seconds, then I would think our event would have spectator appeal also.

So much for Don Swartz reasoning on why he trains middle and distance types in swimming. It is ironic that never since Weissmuller in 1928, has the current "fastest man afloat" won an Olympic swim race. Rather than lose all these colourful crowd-pleasing characters from our sport (and 100 times as many more who simply refuse to go up and down a practice pool 4 hours a day) it seems high time we agitate to have 50 metre freestyle and possibly 50 metre events in all four strokes added to our Olympic programme. Excitement, yes, and more, more people in our sport and more chance for big talent swim types from obscure swim countries to make a showing without every advantage of the world's top swim programmes and big name coaches.

Likewise North American swimming should in this author's opinion, add more 50 yard and 100 yard events and begin calling the fastest times in these events world records (if the world's fastest time) even if not yet official FINA world records. The name of the game is fun and recognition through crowd pleasing swim meets duly recognised by the world record conscious press. Whether or not you agree with the premise it should be fun to see who these sprint types are (or were) in U.S. sprint swimming history.

I have asked Philip S. Harburger, for forty years records chairman of the National Collegiate Athletic Association, to spell it out for us and to trace the progression of U.S. sprint swim times from 1903 to date.

It is interesting to review the improvements made so far in this century in these two sprint events (the 50 and 100 yard freestyle). Strangely enough, the amount of improvement in each of these races has been quite similar: 24·5 per cent for the 50 yard event, and 26·4 per cent for the 100 yards.

In the earliest days of the present century, records in both events were set by Harry Lemoyne of the Brookline (Massachusetts) Swimming Club. He set marks of 27·2 for the 50 in 1904 and 61·4 for the 100 one year earlier.

This 27·2 for 50 yards proved to be a very vulnerable mark, within the next nine years. More improvement took place in those nine years than was registered in the ensuing fifty-seven.

Lemoyne's 27·2 was lowered to 26·6 by Lawrence in 1905, to 25·2 by Charlie Daniels in 1906, to 24·8 by Harry Hebner in 1911, and in 1913, the great Duke Kahanamoku lowered it to 23·4. Volumes have been written about Duke, the peerless Hawaiian, who was years ahead of his time in the sprints. This mark of 23·4 lasted for nine years.

It should be noted that the 50 yard event, while for many years a championship distance (up to 1927) in the AAU, was never actually listed as a record by that body. It was listed as an NCAA record, but on the books of the AAU it was included among "Noteworthy Performances", a classification which was discontinued after the 1957 season.

It was not until August of 1922 that Johnny Weissmuller chopped 6/10ths of a second off the mark to a record 22·8. This was relatively short-lived and the Duke recaptured his sprint title in April 1923 with a 22·6 performance. This record which, while equalled by Peter Fick in 1934, stood for nearly 20 years. This is the longest time that any swimming record has remained on the books in any event in the entire short course programme.

Finally, in March 1943, a young sprinter from Northwestern University, Henry Kozlowski, not only equalled this record in the trials and semifinals of the NCAA Championships but chopped a full $\frac{5}{10}$ of a second off it in the finals to set a mark of 22·1, a record that was to stand for another 11 years.

Dick Cleveland, Ohio State's great sprinter, equalled Kozlowski's mark in 1952 and two years later, chopped off another $\frac{5}{10}$ to bring the listing to 21·9. During the next seven years, this record was equalled by Fred Westphal of the University of Wisconsin, and Harvard's Bruce Hunter. Finally in 1961, the pack had caught up and passed Cleveland's mark as both Frank Legaki of Michigan and Steve Jackman of Minnesota clocked 21·4. Jackman lowered this to 21·1 in 1962 and to 21 flat a year later. Neither of these great sprinters made an Olympic team, indicating that the World's fastest swimmers may not necessarily get to prove it when competing in a long course endurance programme where the shortest event is 100 metres. 100 metres is not a sprint by the physiology limitations measured by oxygen debt.

Steve Clark of Yale was the first to break the 21 second barrier when he hit 20·9 in the NCAA Championships in 1964, a mark that was equalled in 1968 by Zac Zorn of UCLA.

The NCAA Championships saw Dan Frawley of USC lower the record to 20·7 in 1969, and Dave Edgar of Tennessee to 20·5 in 1970, and 20·30 in 1971. John Trembley of Tennessee further lowered the record to 20·23 in 1974, and USC's Joe Bottom to 20·11 in 1975. As previously mentioned, the AAU ceased to list the 50, or other noteworthy performances, after 1957.

In the 100 yard event, the standard sprint distance in the USA, Lemoyne's 61·4 (set in 1903) was blitzed by Charlie Daniels who set a record of 56·0 (1906), 55·4 (1907), and 54·8 (1910). Charles M. Daniels was the first in line of great American swimmers in international events. He won the 100 metre championship in the 1906 Olympic Games in Athens, and again in the fourth Olympiad at London in 1908. His 54·8 record for 100 yards stood for over 11 years. He, like most of the American champions to follow him, did most of his swimming in short course 20 and 25 yard pools.

During this period, Duke Kahanamoku rose to the fore. In beating Daniel's best 100 yard performances, the Duke swam for the greater part over the long course rather than in 25 yard pools. He achieved a time of 54·6 in 1913, later bringing this down, by stages, to 53 flat in 1917. Daniels' 54·8 remained the short course record until the advent of Johnny Weissmuller.

In September 1921, Weissmuller set a standard of 53·2 over the short course, and during the next six years he lowered this successively to 52·4 in 1924, 52·0 in 1925, and finally in April 1927, at Ann Arbor's Union Pool, he beat Buck Sampson to set his famous 51 flat. Weissmuller's 51 second Hundred was the most durable record ever set for the distance. It stood alone for nine years, and was not bettered for nearly 16.

Peter Fick equalled this record in 1936, and in 1942 Howard Johnson of Yale, William Prew of Wayne, and Alan Ford of Yale all equalled this time, yet 51·0 remained a "sound barrier" until January 1943 when Alan Ford achieved 50·7 in January, and 50·6 in February of that year. The following years saw Ford chop this time to 50·1 and finally break the 50 second barrier with a 49·7 performance in March of 1944, a record which he equalled a week later in the NCAA Championships.

This mark remained in force for nearly eight years, and was the last of the long-lived hundred yard marks.

Dick Cleveland of Ohio State University recorded 49·3 and 49·2 in 1952, and this time prevailed until 1956 when Robin Moore, a Stanford football player hit 48·9, a mark which remained on the books for the balance of that decade.

With the advent of the 1960s, Jeff Farrell of the New Haven Swim Club recorded 48·2, and then, in the 1961 AAU Championships at Yale, a schoolboy from Los Altos, California—Steve Clark by name—electrified a capacity audience at the Payne Whitney Exhibition Pool by taking 1 and $\frac{4}{10}$ seconds off this time to clock a phenomenal 46·8.

During the ensuing five years, Clark, now a student at Yale, and Steve Jackman of the University of Minnesota, battled each other with Jackman achieving 46·5 in 1963, which Clark eclipsed the following year with a 46·3 and capped in 1965 with a 45·6 performance. Ken Walsh of Michigan State equalled this time in 1967, and the following year Zac Zorn of UCLA registered 45·3 in the NCAA Championships at Hanover, New Hampshire.

On April 12, 1970, David Edgar of Tennessee lowered the record to 45·1 during the National AAU Championships in Cincinnati, one year later he was the first to break 45 seconds. Andy Coan a Pine Crest (Florida) High school boy broke 44—43·99— in 1975 as a 16-year-old at the Eastern Prep School Championships at Lawrenceville, NJ in February 1975. Jonty Skinner a South African going to Alabama did 43·92, one month later at the Cleveland NCAA's.

In these sprint distances, training methods are not the dominant factor as in the longer distances. Stroke techniques, better pools and pool markings and most particularly the evolution of the turn from grab, to tumble to no hand touch seem to be major factors in the frequency of record breaking.

Is there any limit to this constant improvement of records? The two charts shown indicate that the curves are flattening out in both events, and that the rate of improvement is slowing down. It gets more difficult each year, and yet each year there are new records. It would be a bold person to predict limits of say 19 seconds for the 50, and 43 for the 100, for who, back in the 1920s, would have forseen 20. and 45. in the years to come?

Likewise, the NCAA Championships at Cleveland in 1975 saw teams going under 3 minutes for the 400 yard freestyle relay. This is an indication of the tremendous numbers of sprint swimmers in the United States. Such could be the case throughout the world if we but had sprint events to occupy our sprint minded swimmers.

Nick Thierry, a Canadian Coach-author-statistician writing for *Swimming World* magazine charted a comparison of U.S. high school (14, 15, 16, 17, 18 year olds) sprint swimmers with the older U.S. college swimmers:

> "The United States pre-eminence in sprinting can be attributed to the very large school and college swim programmes. It is estimated that there are about 100,000 participating in high school swimming throughout the United States, while at the NCAA level, the figure is 80,000.
>
> One of the unique events, common to both programmes, is the 50 yard freestyle. No other country, or swim programme has this relatively short, all-out sprint for swimmers in the 15 to 22 age range.
>
> The evolution of both the 50 and 100 yard distances has been virtually parallel since the 1920s. It is worthy of note that the only time the younger high school swimmers surpassed the collegiate ones, was in the early 1960s when Steve Clark bettered both the 50 and 100 yard record. In the 100, his time of 47·7 in 1961 was two tenths faster than the NCAA record. But Steve was to become one of the greatest sprinters of all time.
>
> When will the improvement curve flatten out? Over the past 50 years, the improvement has been pretty well continuous as evidenced by the graph. The conditions under which these events are now held in relation to 50 or 20 years ago have improved remarkably. Consider, that starting blocks and lane lines were not in common usage

until the mid 30s. The design of the bathing suits has gradually decreased in size and weight. The introduction of gutters, non-turbulence lanes, the no-hand touch all had a great effect in an event of relatively short duration. Pool design can still be improved considerably, with the water chemistry (hard or soft) probably being the next area of experimentation.

With even more specialisation, and possibly shorter events, say a 25 yard sprint the times should improve steadily for some years to come."

Thierry could well add that mature men 25 to 30 swimming sprint 50 and 100 yard distances on limited training could continue to swim faster as did Walter Spence who set 100 yards college records as a 35-year-old Rutgers student in 1933 and 1934. It is interesting to speculate on how many college graduates might be able to continue swimming with a light sprint programme compatable with their business careers.

Less you think the author some kind of a sprint nut looking for any easy programme, my success has been in training marathon swimmers. I want swimming and particularly Olympic swimming to be broadened to include the best of all types who would swim. I want a 10,000 metre swim (on the rowing course, before 20,000 spectators) as well as sprint 50s in all four strokes in the Olympic pool.

My great marathon world Champions and world record holders Marty Sinn and Diana Nyad both failed in their efforts to be national winners or even finalists in sprint and middle distance swimming, yet both retained a love of hard training and an ambition to succeed in swimming long after they had been advised to hang it up. To each it was on a last chance when they "struck it rich", winning all at distances of 10, 15, 25, and 40 miles around Manhattan, Atlantic City, Capri to Naples and the Suez Canal. But back to the sprints:

The old formula of a three or four months season, now twelve months with harder and harder work, longer hours and more distance is too simple and the slowdown in timedrop for the shorter distances is a solid indication that you can no longer say a sprinter is merely a well-trained swimmer who happens to swim fast. Psychologically and physically the sprinter must be trained differently or we lose him or lose his edge and thus we actually do have the "so called sprint" (100 m.) won by distance men who "have a kick" as in field and track vernacular of a distance man who also happens to have some speed. Hence a Schollander can train down and win the Olympic 100 m. but a Zorn, Edgar or Trembley need a shorter race and special sprint training.

Certainly the history of U.S. sprint swimming demonstrates the need for shorter distances to be included in world class swim meets.

PROGRESSION OF 100-YARD RECORDS (Short Course)

Compiled by PHILIP S. HARBURGER

61·4 H. Lemoyne, February 14, 1903
56·0 C. M. Daniels, March 23, 1906

54·8 C. M. Daniels, July 4, 1910
53·2 J. Weissmuller, September 24, 1921
52·6 J. Weissmuller, May 27, 1922
52·4 J. Weissmuller, February 17, 1924
52·2 J. Weissmuller, April 24, 1925
52·0 J. Weissmuller, August 10, 1925
51·0 J. Weissmuller, April 5, 1927
P. Fick, April 2, 1936
H. Johnson, February 11, 1942
W. Prew, April 3, 1942
A. Ford, August 14, 1942
50·7 A. Ford, January 10, 1943
50·6 A. Ford, February 13, 1943
50·1 A. Ford, January 29, 1944
49·7 A. Ford, March 18, 1944
A. Ford, March 25, 1944
49·3 R. Cleveland, January 26, 1952
49·2 R. Cleveland, February 23, 1952
R. Cleveland, February 12, 1954
48·9 R. Moore, May 19, 1956
48·2 F. J. Farrell, April 2, 1960
46·8 S. Clark, April 1, 1961
46·5 S. Jackman, March 20, 1963
46·3 S. Clark, March 28, 1964
45·6 S. Clark, April 3, 1965
K. Walsh, March 25, 1967
45·3 Z. Zorn, March 30, 1968
45·2 D. Edgar, April 12, 1970
44·69 D. Edgar, March 27, 1971
43·99 Andy Coan, February 22, 1975
43·92 Jonty Skinner, March 29, 1975

PROGRESSION OF 50-YARD RECORD* (Short Course)

27·2 H. Lemoyne, March 9, 1904
26·6 Lawrence, January 28, 1905
25·2 C. M. Daniels, April 6, 1910
24·8 H. J. Hebner, March 25, 1911
23·4 D. Kahanamoku, August 6, 1913
22·8 J. Weissmuller, August 1, 1922
22·6 D. Kahanamoku, April 26, 1923
P. Fick, May 12, 1934
H. Kozlowski, March 26, 1943
22·1 H. Kozlowski, March 26, 1943
R. Cleveland, February 6, 1952
21·9 R. Cleveland, February 6, 1954
F. Westphal, March 27, 1959
B. Hunter, March 25, 1960
21·4 S. Jackson, March 1, 1961
F. Legaki, March 24, 1961

21·1 S. Jackman, March 30, 1962
21·0 S. Jackman, March 7, 1963
20·9 S. Clark, March 26, 1964
Z. Zorn, March 28, 1968
20·7 D. Frawley, March 27, 1969
20·5 D. Edgar, January 17, 1970
20·30 D. Edgar, March 25, 1971
20·06 J. Trembley, March 28, 1974
*AAU noteworthy performances prior to 1957, NCAA records thereafter.

RECORD PROGRESSION
50-YARD FREESTYLE

HIGH SCHOOL

25·2	Bill Wright	1921
24·0	Pua Kealoha	1923
24·0	Arthur Lindgren	1932
24·0	Matthew Chrostowski	1934
23·8	Matthew Chrostowski	1934
23·6	Matthew Chrostowski	1935
23·5	Robert Delozier	1940
23·5	Edward Garst	1947
23·4	Edward Garst	1947
23·4	Ray Lemaire	1949
23·3	Ronald Gora	1950
23·2	Kenneth Gest	1954
22·9	Kenneth Gest	1954
22·9	Bruce Hunter	1957
22·6	William Baker	1958
22·6	Lance Larson	1958
22·6	Stephen Jackman	1959
22·5	William McGinty	1960
22·5	Marty Hull	1960
22·3	Marty Hull	1960
22·3	Steve Clark	1960
21·8	Steve Clark	1960
21·6	Steve Clark	1961
21·4	Louis Janos	1966
21·2	David Edgar	1968
20·7	John Trembley	1970
20·7	Dave Fairbank	1972
20·5	Joe Bottom	1973
20·2	Andy Coan	1975

NCAA

25·2	S. E. Hoadley	1914
25·0	Edwin Binney	1919
24·4	Edwin Binney	1920
24·0	Edwin Binney	1921
23·9	Arthur Rule	1924
23·8	Harry Lewis	1925
23·6	James Bronson	1926
23·2	John Howland	1930
23·1	Raymond Thompson	1931
22·9	Charles Flackman	1935
22·9	Waldemar Tomski	1939
22·8	Alan Ford	1943
22·6	Henry Kozlowski	1943
22·1	Henry Kozolwski	1943
22·1	Richard Cleveland	1954
22·1	Donald Hill	1954
22·1	Robin Moore	1956
22·0	Robin Moore	1956
21·9	Fred Westphal	1959
21·9	Bruce Hunter	1960
21·4	Steve Jackman	1961
21·4	Frank Legaki	1961
21·1	Steve Jackman	1962
21·0	Steve Jackman	1963
20·9	Steve Clark	1964
20·9	Zac Zorn	1968
20·7	Dan Frawley	1969
20·5	Dave Edgar	1970
20·2	Dave Edgar	1971
20·2	John Trembley	1974

RECORD PROGRESSION 100-YARD FREESTYLE

HIGH SCHOOL

Time	Name	Year
56·8	L. A. Handy	1916
55·4	Pua Kealoha	1923
54·4	George Kojac	1927
54·3	Baker Bryant	1933
54·2	Baker Bryant	1933
54·0	Matthew Chrostowski	1934
53·9	Matthew Chrostowski	1934
53·4	Matthew Chrostowski	1935
53·2	Matthew Chrostowski	1935
52·6	Henry Kozlowski	1941
51·5	Ronald Gora	1950
51·2	Richard Hanley	1955
50·9	Elton Follett	1957
50·7	Fred Rounds	1957
50·4	Peter Sintz	1958
50·2	Lance Larson	1958
50·1	William McGinty	1959
49·6	William McGinty	1959
48·9	Steve Clark	1960
48·4	Steve Clark	1960
47·8	Steve Clark	1961
47·7	Steve Clark	1961
47·7	Robert Jamison	1966
47·6	Robert Jamison	1967
47·6	Rick Eagleston	1967
47·4	Rick Eagleston	1967
47·0	Robert Jamison	1967
46·6	Robert Jamison	1967
46·0	Mark Spitz	1968
45·6	Mark Spitz	1968
45·0	Joe Bottom	1973
44·0	Andy Coan	1975

NCAA

Time	Name	Year
56·4	Hal Vollmer	1916
55·6	D. L. Jones	1921
54·8	D. L. Jones	1923
54·6	James Bronson	1925
53·4	James Bronson	1926
53·2	Albert Schwartz	1929
52·8	George Kojac	1930
52·4	George Kojac	1931
51·6	Walter Spence	1933
51·6	Walter Spence	1934
51·6	William Prew	1941
51·6	Howard Johnson	1942
51·1	Edward Hall	1942
50·7	Alan Ford	1943
49·7	Alan Ford	1944
49·3	Richard Cleveland	1952
49·2	Richard Cleveland	1954
49·0	Rex Aubrey	1956
48·9	Robin Moore	1956
48·6	Bruce Hunter	1960
47·9	Ray Padovan	1961
47·0	Michael Austin	1962
46·3	Steve Clark	1964
46·1	Steve Clark	1965
45·6	Ken Walsh	1967
45·3	Zac Zorn	1968
44·5	Dave Edgar	1971
43·9	Jonty Skinner	1975

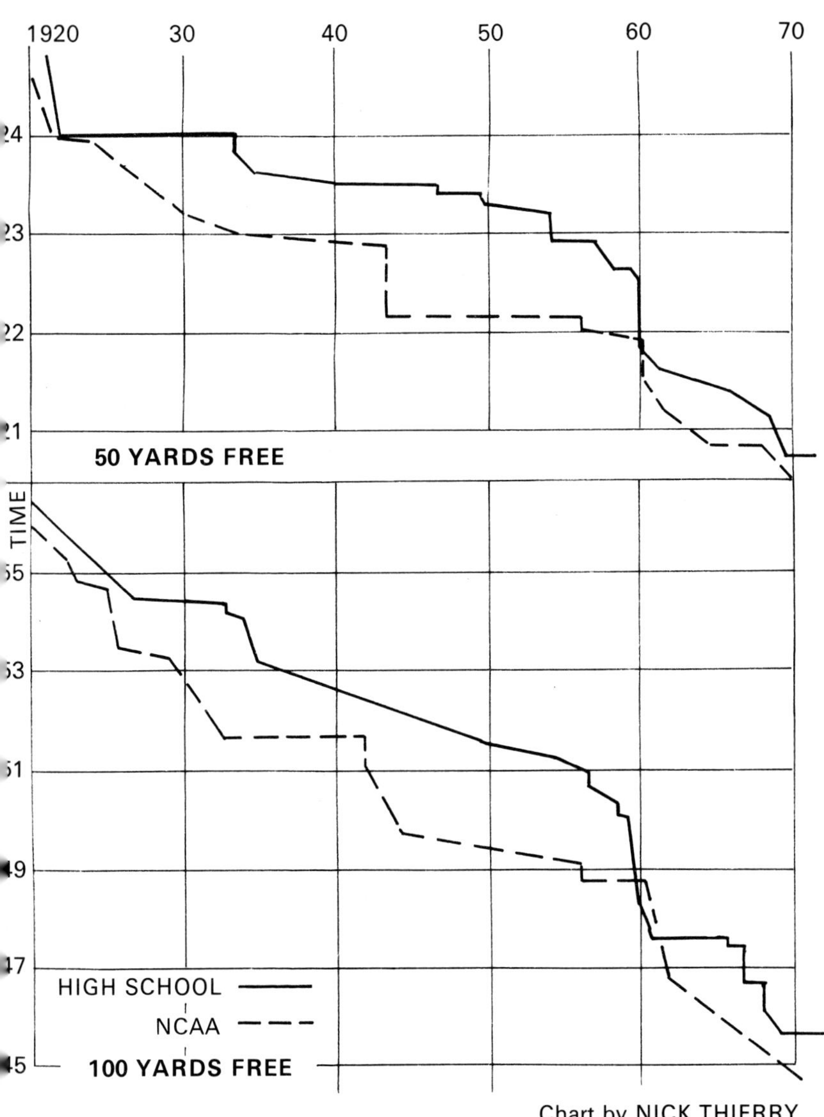

Chart by NICK THIERRY

10. The Future

If you have glossed over the preceding list of U.S. record holders please examine it a little more closely. There are some magnificent sprinters in the list. Ford, Cleveland, Clark, Austin, Walsh, Zorn in the latter years and Kojac, Kealoha, Schwartz and Spence in the 1920s and 1930s. These men in their time were the fastest freestyle sprinters in the world and yet an absolutely amazing fact emerges from the list; of all the swimmers recorded here only one has ever won an Olympic 100 metres freestyle title, Mark Spitz. Many have placed and some have assisted in winning relays but only Spitz has won as an individual.

Kealoha placed second in 1920 at Antwerp, Kojac placed fourth in 1928 at Amsterdam, Schwartz managed a third in 1932 at Los Angeles and Thompson came in sixth. Alan Ford swam a second at London in 1948 and Richard Hanley a sixth in 1956. Lance Larson was the closest of seconds at Rome in that disputed finish in 1960 and Hunter finished fourth in the same race. Mike Austin managed a sixth in 1964 at Tokyo and in 1968 at Mexico Spitz finished third and Walsh second. Mark Spitz placed first at Munich.

If these great stars have only managed a placing now and then, where have the winners come from and just as importantly why have the school champions failed to produce winning form at the Olympics?

The list below shows what has happened in the American sprint scene since 1905. It is estimated that by 1985 the record for the 100 yards freestyle will be approaching 42 seconds, but from this point on the improvement will slow dramatically. The 100 metres mark should be in the forty-eights. The average improvement over the past sixty years is close to 1·8 seconds a decade or point 2 of a second each year, for the 100 yards.

Improvement in seconds for the 100 yards men's freestyle in ten yearly periods:

Year	Record	Swimmer	Improvement	Some Technical Additions
1905	61·4 sec.	Lemoyne		
1915	54·8 sec.	Daniels	6·6 sec.	rope lanes
1925	52·0 sec.	Weissmuller	2·8 sec.	first modern crawl stroke
1935	51·0 sec.	Weissmuller	1·0 sec.	refined crawl stroke
1945	49·7 sec.	Ford	1·3 sec.	weight training
1955	49·2 sec.	Cleveland	0·5 sec.	tumble turns, pool improvement
1965	46·1 sec.	Clark	3·1 sec.	sloping blocks, better lanes
1975	43·9 sec.	Coan	2·2 sec.	improved swim suits, grab start
1985	42·0 sec.	predicted time	1·9 sec.	

To be able to swim 100 yards in 42 seconds a more specific approach will have to be undertaken. Super sprinters will have to be selected by testing or by elimination and they will have to train for distances up to the 100 yards and very little else. In this respect we will have to start imitating the sprint training of the great American negro track stars. The reason is logical physiologically. The neuro-muscular patterns of sprinting are specific to each speed in sprinting, so if we wish to move at two yards per second we should do the bulk of our work at, or in excess of, this speed. This underlines the old saying that sprinting makes sprinters.

A failing in today's sprint schedules is that sprinters do not sprint hard enough often enough. Swimmers and coaches are satisfied with speeds approaching 1·7 or 1·8 yards per second for example when fewer sprints at speeds in excess of 2·0 yards per second would produce a better end result. In very short sprints speeds of 2·2 yards per second or greater should be attempted. A point that has been missed by many but now must be incorporated in future sprint schedules, is that some training must be done at faster than race pace and sections of the stroke (kicking, pulling) have also to be practised at a rate which will be faster than used in the race, over short distances. Kick practice on the kick board will have to be done at a tempo faster than the actual kick used in the event. Likewise "arms only" training will have to be done so the arms move faster and do more work than they will in the same time and distance of the all-out race.

Overall one essential must be dominant. In all the overspeed practices of stroke, kick or pull, your natural stroke must not be altered except in tempo, for if you have developed your technique over the seasons and it is efficient, do not alter it unless advised by the coach. What we are now trying to do is take your stroke and condition it to produce a greater output of effective power without fade over short distances. It is not much use shooting for 100 yards in 50 seconds if you cannot manage 50 yards in 25 seconds or 25 yards in 12½ seconds, so first of all we have to develop the speed required and once this is achieved extend that speed as far as you as an individual are capable.

If you continually train at a speed slower than your race target time your final performance will be slower. Overspeed training is very stressful, not much yardage is covered and it is very time-consuming for coach and pupil. Overspeed training is more beneficial for the advanced sprinter and not so much for the novice who is still mastering the skill of swimming. Overspeed requires determination in giant doses from the sprinter and intelligent application from the coach.

The reasons why the sprints in the overspeed training must be of very short duration are both mental and physical. Psychological because the student can brain-wash himself into sprinting across the pool twenty or thirty times at a speed faster than 2 yards or metres per second, he can force himself to do it probably several times a week without mental rejection. He will return for more but the sprinter has not yet emerged who will back up day after day for repeat 100 metres or even 50 metres all-out sprints without souring to his task. I am now referring to all-out speed on all sprints every sprint being an attempt on the personal best time. Since the ultra-short distances at all-out speed will be acceptable to the true sprinter it is up to the ingenuity of the coach to alter, motivate and scheme to keep this level of acceptance high.

The energy for sprinting stems from two sources, depending upon the duration and intensity of the spirit, aerobic and anaerobic metabolism in the muscular contractions. The liberation of aerobic energy is dependent upon oxygen being delivered to the working muscles through the cardiovascular system. In spurts of intensive sprinting this supply of aerobic energy is inadequate. Most of the energy in sprinting stems from anaerobic sources and this in turn produces the phenomenon of oxygen debt. There are two sources of anaerobic energy within the muscle and this is a very important fact for the construction of the overspeed swimming schedule.

The first source, phosphogen, is available only for the first twelve to sixteen seconds of maximum muscular effort and fortunately this energy source is rapidly replaced if a short rest is taken. In an effort of such short duration there is no build-up of lactic acid, the pain producer, the speed killer. If the all-out sprint takes longer than sixteen seconds the limits of both anaerobic energy sources is approached. The second source of anaerobic energy, glycolysis, provides most of the energy for the additional period of the sprint but unfortunately glycolysis produces lactic acid. In prolonged sprinting or in frequent sprints without adequate rest intervals, it produces pain and extreme muscular fatigue such as sprinters experience in the legs, arms and chest towards the latter stages of an all-out 100 metres.

Repeated sprints of sixteen seconds or longer produce and accumulate large amounts of lactic acid in the muscles and in the circulating blood. The process of elimination of this lactic acid is lengthy and may even persist for the duration of the training session. I have not been able to verify but I strongly suspect, the circulating lactic acid has an inhibiting influence on the brain which in turn produces signals that indicate the work output is to slow down. I feel lactic acid is nature's way of forcing on the brake in order to protect the organs and systems. As with all things in nature there is a flexibility, a tolerance, and it is largely within this tolerance region the sprinter works. He must often work towards the upper limits of this tolerance zone to experience training pain and to learn to swim with it. The super sprint schedule must, in part, be constructed of maximum work which is short enough to avoid glycolysis and the accompanying lactic acid accumulation.

Today's sprint programme should not completely cancel out the better aspects of the accepted type of work we have been doing but we must incorporate more ultra sprinting, possibly do less mileage and introduce specific land exercises. I think it is now generally accepted one does not have to perform daily training stints of 15,000 metres to 20,000 metres in order to excel over fifty or one hundred yards. The programme tailored to suit today's developing sprint champion should be made up of sprint-endurance type training in the morning session and ultra sprint training in the afternoon. Some advantages of the ultra sprint system are:

* Psychologically the team realises they have been recognised as sprinters, that they are specialists training for a sprint, and there is not much likelihood of long, hard endurance-type work being placed on them. A large number of today's squads have very little idea for what they are specifically training. Most are in training to become better swimmers. In the ultra sprint programme the sprinter knows that all his kicking, pulling and training drills are aimed at building up enough power to last 20 or 50 seconds in the big event.
* The excitement of a dozen or more team mates sprinting across the pool is so intense the pupils will accept the coach's request for an all-out effort, the duration of pain being so short, the fun so all-consuming.
* The skill of sprinting is enriched.
* More worthwhile strokes are performed in a given period of time.
* The coach has better control and co-operation in the smaller area with willing students.
* Starts, turns, push-offs and finishes are performed at race speed.
* Breath holding techniques and breath holding endurance is mastered.

One observation of "across the pool" interval training is the rest intervals are lengthy in comparison with the time swum, for instance, 10 seconds of maximum work and 10 seconds rest. Research has shown if the resting time is too long the benefit of the work will be eroded, so care must be taken when allotting rest intervals. However it is during the rest section that the greatest stimulus to improvement in the heart's ability to pump blood occurs, and the greatest volume of blood per beat is pumped. The rest also enhances a faster absorbtion of oxygen, the continued vasodilation of the arterial vessels as well as a partial recovery from the lactic acid build-up. In ultra-short sprints of maximum effort the rest intervals between sprints should not be greater than two to one, that is ten seconds of work and twenty seconds of rest. Since lactic acid builds up faster when continuous work is being done as against a lesser amount accumulated with interval training, the benefits of this type of training are many.

There is something very satisfying and exciting about "across the pool" sprints which one rarely finds in the normal training session. Most coaches do incorporate ultra short sprints in the programme but usually only towards the end of the season's training, when the pupil is approaching final taper down. I have dissected the training programmes of many top sprinters but have not found one where the sprinter has persevered with the ultra-short sprint system for a lengthy period. In Australia, world record holder Michael Wenden came closest to this system with many sessions never exceeding sprints in excess of fifty metres.

As a preliminary to the possible introduction of an ultra-short sprint system as a permanent feature, I worked five girls with sprinting potential as a test team for a period of six weeks. Sprints with a duration of sixteen seconds or less constituted eighty per cent of the workout. Since the test was conducted at the end of the summer season when it was anticipated the sprinters had reached their top, the improvement was significant.

Thegirls trained with the junior squad of a morning, the total work being 6,000 metres. The morning schedule followed these lines:

1. 30 × 50 metres sprints every 50 seconds at 90 per cent effort.
2. 10 × 100 metres legs tied efforts every 2 minutes.
3. 5 × 200 continuous medleys at 80 per cent effort.
4. 10 × 100 metres kick sprints every 2 minutes.
5. 5 × 200 metres efforts every 2 minutes at 90 per cent effort
6. 20 × 25 metres sprints in the medley order every 20 seconds.

The afternoon training was as follows:

1. 20 sprints across the pool departing every 20 seconds and working at 1·7 yards a second for the 20 yards width. This was the technique warm up. This work was all freestyle or butterfly.
2. 10 sprints across the pool and back (40 yards) working at 1·9 yards a second, departing every 80 seconds (20 seconds work, 60 seconds rest)
3. 20 × 20 yards kick sprints each sprinter attempting to achieve her very best time on each sprint. The fade off in this section was noticeable. One sprint every 40 seconds.
4. 500 metres of free choice over the long course to allow for muscle relaxation.
5. 20 × 20 yards legs tied sprints each sprinter aiming for 1·7 yards a second departing every 30 seconds.
6. This last section was varied according to the needs of the pupils. At times we would attempt to better the world record for the 100 yards by doing 5 sprints across the pool, departing every 20 seconds and totalling the times. We would repeat this exercise 5 times and the sprinters were required to go faster each time. Each girl would have 6 minutes rest between each attempt.

Or

We would attempt dive sprints of 25 metres aiming at speeds greater than 2 metres a second. This standard was never achieved but the girls, by constantly striving reached speeds of 1·9 metres a second.

* The system required one or two extra timekeepers and an alert coach.
* Care was taken so one sluggish girl did not pull down the spirit of the system.

* The afternoon schedule was altered often but the above workout was typical.
* The results at the end of the six weeks over 50 metres long course were:
  Carmel Walker, 12 years, from 31·3 to 29·7 seconds
  Lee Anne Packman, 12 years, from 31·8 to 29·8 seconds
  Fiona McAlister, 14 years, from 30·2 to 28·8 seconds
  Lisa Curry, 12 years, from 31·1 to a new state record of 28·3 seconds
  Jeanette Potts, 12 years, from 32·0 to 29·8 seconds
* Five "control" boys working in the general squad and not on the special programme also improved, the average improvement being point 8 of a second. Special note should be made of Sandra Bright, 14 years, a butterfly swimmer with outstanding endurance but lacking in early speed. On a schedule of ultra-short sprinting across the pool in the afternoon sessions Sandra's speed improved dramatically (her 50 metres butterfly went from 33·0 to 31·3). She later annexed the National Age Title for the 200 metres butterfly in 2:20·6, a record.

Velocity calculations for sprint distances in yards and metres per second

Velocity yds/m per sec	1·2	1·3	1·4	1·5	1·6	1·7	1·8	1·9	2·0	2·1	2·2
Time 20 yds/m	16·67	15·38	14·29	13·33	12·50	11·76	11·11	10·53	10·00	9·52	9·09
Time 25 yds/m	20·83	19·23	17·86	16·67	15·63	14·71	13·89	13·16	12·50	11·90	11·36
Time 50 yds/m	41·67	38·46	35·71	33·33	31·25	29·41	27·78	26·32	25·00	23·83	22·73
Time 100 yds/m	83·33	76·92	71·43	66·67	62·50	58·82	55·56	52·63	50·00	47·62	45·45

Index